The Natural Navigator Pocket Guide

About the Author

Tristan Gooley set up his natural navigation school, The Natural Navigator, after studying and practising the art for over ten years. His passion for the subject stems from hands-on experience. He has led expeditions in five continents, climbed mountains in Europe, Africa and Asia, sailed across oceans and piloted small aircraft to Africa and the Arctic. He is the only living person to have both flown and sailed solo across the Atlantic. Tristan is a Fellow of both the Royal Institute of Navigation and the Royal Geographical Society and is the Vice Chairman of Trailfinders. He lives with his wife and two sons in West Sussex.

The
Natural
Navigator
Pocket Guide

TRISTAN GOOLEY

6 8 10 9 7

Previously published as *The Natural Navigator*

This abridged edition published in 2011 by Virgin Books,
an imprint of Ebury Publishing, a Random House Group Company

Copyright © Tristan Gooley 2011

Illustration on page 115 © Ocean Planet/Smithsonian
Illustration on page 66 © Science Museum/SSPL
All other illustrations © Ruth Murray
Designed by Lindsay Nash

The Random House Group Limited Reg. No. 954009

Addresses for companies within the Random House Group can be
found at www.randomhouse.co.uk

A CIP catalogue record for this book
is available from the British Library

ISBN 9780753539859

Printed and bound in India by Replika Press Pvt. Ltd.

To buy books by your favourite authors and register for offers, visit
www.randomhouse.co.uk

For Sophie, Benedict and Vincent

Contents

INTRODUCTION

The Art of Natural Navigation

Natural navigation is the art of finding your way by using nature. It consists mainly of the rare skill of being able to determine direction without the aid of tools or instruments and only by reference to natural clues including the sun, the moon, the stars, the land, the sea, the weather, the plants and the animals.

Natural navigation is an ancient art, borne from an era when there were no alternatives. Natural selection dictated that those animals and humans unable to work out a way of getting to where they needed to be in order to survive did not contribute to the next generation's gene pool. Evolutionary theory tends to focus on the physical: as a general rule, the faster the animal, the better its chances, but in the race for survival speed in the wrong direction was a fast way to lose out. We now know that we exist in part because our ancestors learned how to navigate, even if we do not yet fully understand how they did so.

Ancient journeys can enrich contemporary ones, because the ancients learned to read their surroundings with more skill than most modern travellers can. They have much to teach, but it is not laid out in ancient textbooks. Some of the pieces of the jigsaw come from oral traditions, or even the very earliest images etched in stone.

The ancient Egyptian god Horus may not help us to navigate directly, but the myths that surround him illuminate for us the way in which the ancient Egyptians perceived the sky. Horus took the form of a falcon and his two eyes were the sun and moon. He had injured his left eye, the moon, and was sometimes blind in it, but even when he could see it was always weaker than his right eye, the sun. This helps demonstrate the Egyptian familiarity with the moon's

[2]

phases as it moved from an invisible new moon to a full moon.

Religious texts are another ancient source. They exist either as a reflection of reality or an attempt to explain it, depending on your viewpoint, but either way they yield valuable information about early journeys, perspectives and methods. The Quran refers to the use of rivers, the sun, moon, stars, landmarks and shadows as means of navigating and encourages this: 'Surely in this there are signs for men of understanding.' [3]

Why Navigate at All?

War and conquest have been motives both for great journeys and pioneering navigation. The hunger for new territory can be found behind many of the great expeditions, from the ancient Egyptian ruler Necho II, who wanted to see canals forced through land and sent ships to circumnavigate Africa, and on down to the European scramble for colonies in the late nineteenth century.

For others, the desire to travel has come from intellectual curiosity. Solon was an Ancient

Greek who travelled to Egypt on a sightseeing trip, while the Roman poet Manilius wrote of his astonishment that people would travel to see art and temples rather than to stand and wonder at the volcano of Mt Etna. Other motives have been a little earthier. Long before the Pacific explorers of the eighteenth century returned with tales of the beauty of the women and their generosity with their sexual favours, new lands have hinted at the possibility of sexual adventure.

[4]   Some journeys are a temporary flight from responsibility. The great natural navigators of the Micronesian island of Puluwat have long had a habit of getting drunk and then sailing to the neighbouring island of Pikelot:

> 'A minimum of equipment and any available food is loaded aboard and they depart, singing and shouting as they work their way across the lagoon and out of the pass, while their wives and other sober souls scowl their disapproval on shore.'

We travel not only to escape, consume and copulate, but also to think and create. Jean Jacques Rousseau wrote, 'When I stay in one place I can hardly think at all.'

The Silent Revolution

One of the earliest glimpses of the compass can be found in a French poem written by Guy de Provins at the start of the thirteenth century. And so we witness the start of the silent, technical revolution in wayfaring, whereby an individual with previously valuable knowledge of the stars, the sun, the moon and the sea itself is to be usurped by an 'ugly brown stone' to which iron sticks. And now the compass itself is having its supremacy tested by the irrepressible rise of satellite navigation.

[5]

The impact of this revolution is given perspective by looking at the changing role of the navigator in society. In many societies there are cultural links between maturity and an ability to navigate. Young Australian Aboriginal men are expected to set out on a journey of some length as part of the rite of passage to adulthood. In the Pacific, navigators were traditionally afforded an elevated status in the social hierarchy, not far below that of a priest. Their knowledge was passed down from father to son and jealously guarded.

In our industrialised society, the navigator is

in danger of losing the place afforded to those with valuable skills and becoming viewed as just one more machine operator. The job often disappears altogether as the task of navigating by computer is assimilated into a broader job: there are still pilots in the cockpits of aircraft who navigate effectively, but very few 'navigators' left in these cockpits.

Why Navigate Naturally?

[6]   Asking yourself the question, 'which way am I looking?' can present the key to unlock the natural world. Using our senses and mind to answer it can lead to thoughts, connections and ideas that are as exciting as any journey that follows.

Natural navigation is one of the rarest arts on the planet, but it has not yet disappeared altogether. We tend to see it primarily in relation to our understanding of how earlier cultures looked at the world. It is common to encounter the notion that the degree to which the ancients were connected to the natural world indicates their lack of sophistication. We consider our need to lead lives that leave no time for contemplation of our physical environment as superior, but in doing so we often fail to recognise what has been lost.

The second way in which natural navigation has endured is as a survival technique. Though there are very few books on the subject itself, it surfaces in the hundreds of books that cover survival skills. Survival is by definition a desperate and urgent business and this approach strips out almost all that is fascinating in the subject. Survivalists are not going to spend time contemplating the ancient Greek astronomer Hipparchus or arcane relationships between beaches and the moon.

A very common question is whether being able to navigate naturally is a necessary skill. Since it is quite possible to get through our daily lives without any knowledge of this most ancient of arts, the answer must be 'no'. However, it is also true that we can get by in life without any knowledge of music, art, drama or history. So a better answer to this question is perhaps that it does not matter if you are walking to the newsagent or sailing across an ocean, natural navigation can provide a unique insight into the world around you.

Safety remains the top priority in any journey

and the techniques in this book are recom-
mended for use in a complementary way and
not instead of navigational instruments. All
normal instruments and maps should still be
carried and used to ensure safe journeys.

Getting Ready

Familiarity is the foundation stone of all early
navigation experiences. Very young children
like to keep parents or home within sight. As
[8]   the child grows older, the distance from their
comfort zone that they are prepared, and able,
to travel grows steadily. By the time of adulthood the process is so intrinsic that little
thought is given to understand 'how' it works.
From a familiarity with surroundings, a series
of associations develops, most of which are
logical and useful. But humans are also prone
to making incorrect assumptions. Natural navigation is therefore about effectively combining
observation and deduction.

We all learn to 'read' our home areas as a
series of recognisable landmarks, from road
junctions to where we are in relation to a river.
There does not appear to be any bias towards

either natural or manmade landmarks, only towards what works. This adaptability can also be seen in the animal kingdom: bees look for patterns that they recognise, regardless of whether they are natural or manmade.

Here, then, is the first system for wayfaring without instruments: all we need to do is become familiar with the landmarks of an area and then remember where they are, relative to each other and our destination. There are only two real flaws to this method: landmark navigation only works on land and if you are already familiar with [9] an area. Our perception of the world around us is subjective. We each develop a unique memory map of an area, which will vary significantly from that of any other person.

There is a way of describing locations that does not require familiarity and is not subjective, but a new way of describing places is needed to use it. In fact, it is a new language.

Taming Conventions

Every location in the world can be described in terms of its direction from a known point and the distance from that point. The international

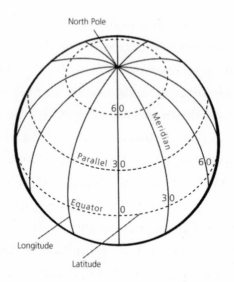

navigational language that has become most prevalent is to describe location by referring how far north or south a place is from the Equator (latitude) and how far east or west it is from Greenwich, London (longitude). Direction is described by cutting the circle of all possible directions up into 360 degrees, starting at the direction of the 'north', and working clockwise all the way back round to it.

The use of 'degrees' can appear cold and mathematical. But the concept remains a natural one: 10 degrees is simply one thirty-sixth of a circle, whether it is measured by a sextant, compass or an outstretched fist. The conventions over distance are more convoluted, but here too we find roots in nature. The 'mile' stems from the Roman term '*mille passus*', denoting 1,000 paces, and the metre was defined by the French in 1791 as one ten-millionth of the distance from the North Pole to the Equator, via Paris.

All of this amounts to a kind of shorthand for communicating directions and distances. There is nothing that makes any one method of short-hand inherently more correct than another. If you find it easier to discuss direction among friends in terms relative to a local landmark and to communicate distance using paces, then not even the Royal Institute of Navigation can call that wrong.

Wherever I have used the established conventions in this book, it is because they stand the best chance of being meaningful, not because they represent the beauty in the subject. Natural navigators should feel free to translate these conventions into the language they find most comfortable.

A Sense of Connection

Learning to navigate naturally forces us to re-examine the ways we connect to our physical environment, how our senses are pivotal to effective natural navigation and how they in turn define our experience and understanding. Sensual awareness is critical to finding our way without instruments, but it is also important if we do not want to be denied some of the texture of a journey.

[12]   *Sight*

Our eyes feed far more detailed information to our brains than we can possibly process and so a

When you first looked at this picture, did you notice the curve in the path or the subtle change in shade from one side of the path to the other?

filtration takes place. Our brain allows us to focus on what seems most important, but the process is not perfect for two key reasons. The first is that there are biases in our view of the world. We are much more sensitive to shape than we are to colour, for example.

Secondly, because we are no longer primarily concerned with survival, it is often necessary to unlearn our instinctive response to the world we see. The modern natural navigator must stop, look and think about the environment in a way that even our most naturally astute ancestors may not have done.

[13]

Smell and Taste

The pioneering Australian navigator Harold Gatty referred to the smells of rosemary off Spain and orange groves off the islands of Cape Verde. It is something that all sailors who have spent time away from land will have experienced. There is a well-known connection between smell and memory, which is made more poignant by the fact that our sense of smell peaks in middle age and then deteriorates as we get older.

The human ability to use smell to understand

territory is weak compared to most animals, but not non-existent. There is a street market on North End Road in west London, which sells a lot of fruit and fresh produce. The street smells different at different times of the day and year. Early on a winter day there is no way of telling how close you are to the market by smell, but late on a summer day the scent of overripe fruit that has been trampled on the roads and pavements carries several hundred metres downwind.

[14]   This relationship between temperature and smell can be used in a rural context too. There is a distinct difference between the smell of open country and woodland and this can be used to find your way out of the woods if you pick it up on the breeze. In wilderness areas most unusual smells will be a clue to humans, other animals or changes in the environment. The desert smells very clean until humans, animals or water are introduced, all three often coming together at an oasis and giving off a relatively strong smell.

Our taste buds are most sensitive to sweet, sour, salt and bitterness. Nearly everything else is determined by our sense of smell. Different meats taste the same if we hold our nose and so it is best to think of the two senses, taste and smell, as working in tandem.

It is possible, with care, to tell whether a watercourse is freshwater or tidal seawater from its salinity. If you are following a stream hoping to emerge from the wild nearer the coast then this may be of some help.

Sound

Sounds form an integral part of a landscape and journey. This can be shown by the way blind [15] people use a stick for the sense of touch, but also to gauge echoes. On my courses I ask a volunteer to walk in silence, with their hands behind their back and their eyes shut, towards a wall until they feel uncomfortably close. Next I ask them to do the same thing whilst making a constant noise, '*la la la la la*'. They typically manage to get more than a foot closer to the wall when making the noise.

This is the principle behind radar and echo sounders, but it has been used in a practical way long before that. The timed echo of a whistle in Puget Sound was used by a navigator in fog to gauge how far the cliffs were and the timbre of the echo gave clues as to the exact bluff or cliff off which it was bouncing. Another example of using our ears to navigate comes from F. Spencer Chapman's experiences with the Inuit in Greenland. He watched them navigate their way in kayaks along the coast in fog, using the unique song of each male snow bunting to identify where their home fjörd was.

The Australian Aboriginals have long used their ears to understand journeys in a unique way. Their 'songlines' mapped the territory around them in a series of songs and stories, some of which are still in use today. Each part of a song corresponds with an important landmark, such as a ridge or source of water. By recalling the right song the land can be navigated with greater familiarity and, thanks to the sense of hearing, the memory and experience of their journeys lives on beyond their destination.

[16]

Touch

The sensations of the ground underfoot have always been a delight for sailors returning to shore, but also for those who have been on the ice for too long. Scott felt this acutely: 'A lot could be written on the delight of setting foot on rock after fourteen weeks of snow and ice.'

The contrasts are often much subtler. The difference between one side of a ridge and another may have been generated by millions of years of erosive forces, but that may only translate into the tiniest change underfoot, from a coarse to a fine scree. There are some paths that feel different on each side, despite looking identical.

When there is a harsh ground frost the sense of touch can sometimes help. Paths are usually [17] marginally higher or lower than the surrounding ground and when warmer daytime breezes come to thaw the ground, paths tend to retain or lose their frost at a different rate from the ground on either side. It is sometimes possible to follow a lower path, even in the dark, by keeping the crunchy feel of frozen grass underfoot.

Sensory Deprivation

It is not always what we can feel, but what we cannot, that triggers our senses. The Antarctic explorer Frederick Cook sensed danger from still-ness. When we become accustomed to a sensation, like a biting wind, its absence can make us uneasy, a prompt for us to be alert to the fact that something in our environment has changed.

Not all sensations are external. We are more likely to be able to understand where we have travelled if we walk it ourselves than if we are carried. The feeling of muscle contractions can give clues about direction and distance. This 'kinaesthetic' ability is something that we have all experienced in a general sense: we can tell the difference in feeling in our legs between a one-kilometre walk and a ten-kilometre one.

[18]

When important natural clues disappear, then the senses must be relied on to their fullest. If the sun vanishes behind thick cloud, it does not mean

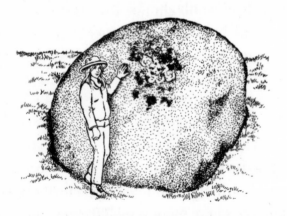

When the sun disappears behind clouds it is possible to 'remember' where it was by touching two sides of a large boulder.

that all trace of it has vanished. It is possible to 'remember' where it was by touching two sides of a large boulder. One side will retain warmth for a long time after the sun has gone in, the exact length of time depending on the type of rock.

Time

Although not one of the five senses, time is integral to navigation. Everyone who has gone a few weeks without wearing a watch will likely have noticed that their 'inner clock' starts to run more accurately. Experiments going back to 1935 have demonstrated this ability. Humans deprived of all external time clues are able to gauge time accurately with only about a ten-minute error per twenty-four hours.

[19]

Time is part of nature. Water clocks were used in Babylonian times, and sundials could be found in Rome from the third century BCE. Use of the sun to gauge time can still be seen in cultures that do not rely upon modern technology. In the Kalahari Desert, the Gwi tribe measure time in days and fractions of days by pointing to where the sun will be at the time they mean on the day in question.

Modern walkers still measure distance using time. The question, 'How far is it?' from one walker to the next is often answered by, 'An hour.' Scott used a combination of time and knowledge of his animals to mark distance in the Antarctic: 'We are at Number Fourteen Pony Camp, only two pony marches from One Ton Depot.'

Learning to understand nature takes time. It is not something best approached with firm schedules or a particular deadline. Natural navigators will regularly set out hopeful of returning [20] with some new knowledge in one area and return with something else. A lot of the enjoyment of the subject is to be had in lateral thought and mental detours. This is helped enormously by an old-fashioned approach to time. It is much better to go for a walk that happens to take half an hour, than to go for a half-hour walk.

It is time for us to take the first steps.

CHAPTER 1

Vale and Dune: The Land

The most common method for finding direction on land relies on the traveller's familiarity with the landscape itself. This is known as landmark navigation.

From ancient wilderness to supermarket aisles, few people have reached adulthood without some memories of disorientation and the accompanying fear. At the heart of this experience is the realisation that straying from family or venturing away from home needs to be accompanied by the ability to get back. This is one of the simplest of navigational philosophies: if you can find your way back safely, knowledge about the direction of the outward journey is a lot less critical and can often be dispensed with.

Trail blazing is the process of marking a path at various points, creating markers that then assist on the return journey and on subsequent visits. This takes many forms, from leaving chalk markings to broken branches. Signposts are themselves just highly evolved trail blazes.

In most areas of open country it is possible to find examples of people changing the appearance of the landscape, from the *inuksuit*, [22] the mounds of stones left by the Inuit in the Arctic to those left by Scott in the Antarctic. At other times and places a different solution might be used. The Aboriginals of Australia traditionally lit spinifex grass fires that indicated the way from a considerable distance.

Trail blazes, cairns and fires have been set up to stand out from nature for a good reason. Finding direction by reading the land can be difficult and even dangerous. In many ways modern navigational tools do not make the task of reading the land easier; if anything they have made this much more difficult by conditioning the traveller's focus away from the land itself.

Reading the Land

There are two key foundation stones to reading the land. One is learning to interpret the effects of sun, wind and water. The other is gaining an appreciation of the importance of scale.

Useful clues can be on a distant horizon or just centimetres away. This means that it is necessary to keep the senses scouring, shifting focus constantly, which requires conscious effort, but yields plenty of rewards. The natural navigator puts more into a land journey than [23] other travellers, but returns with a basketful of observations and sensations that pass others by.

From this spot there may be clues in the sky, in the shape of the land, in the trees, in the lichen on the fencepost or even in the mud you are standing in.

Hills, Rocks and Rivers

The search for distant and closer clues should start from the best position possible: this usually means finding the highest vantage point.

A good view will help to form a picture of the shape, the patterns and grain of the land itself. High ground will tell a story of geological formation and erosion. The South Downs, mounds of chalk that have determinedly weathered erosion over millions of years, runs broadly west to east, near parallel to the English south coast. Once this alignment is understood, one can make simple deductions. If the sea can be seen, then there must be some south in the view, but if the land slopes away continuously to low country it must be close to north.

The character of the hills themselves can also be influenced by aspect. The southern side of any northern hemisphere range will experience a greater variety of temperature than the northern side. In winter, the southern side may go through repeated frost and thaw cycles, while the northern side, hidden from the warmth of the sun, remains consistently frozen. This leads to greater erosive forces on the southern side, often giving it a different look and feel.

[24]

On a smaller scale, burrowing animals like moles tend to prefer damper mud that can be found on the shaded slopes and this can lend a darker, rougher appearance. Sometimes the general effect is detectable from a distance, but the detail can only be seen close up. In the summer in particular, shaded areas retain moisture longer: inspecting these dark patches close up in turn will reveal much smaller culprits, like ants enjoying the ground that has been kept shady, cool and moist.

Hills and rivers have a symbiotic relationship; [25] water is channelled by land but then carves into that land over time. It is impossible to understand one without the other. While the Pennines run north–south, there are rivers in the Pennines, like the Ure and its accompanying valley of Wensleydale, that run west–east off them.

Water, in its solid form of ice, has shaped large areas of land through the movement of glaciers and ice sheets. Within the broader effects, more distinct patterns can sometimes be read. The shape of the land can betray the direction of the long-departed ice and can in turn be used to find direction. In County Armagh, Northern Ireland, there are a series of

Direction of ice flow

Retreating ice sculpts the land and leaves clues to direction.

[26]

small hills known as 'drumlins' that have been shaped by the retreating ice and appear elongated along the axis that the ice has flowed, in this case south–north.

Where there is little water, the geology becomes of greater importance. The Bedouin of the Arabian Peninsula come to know intimately the shape of rock outcropping and to recognise patterns where others would see none.

Puddles

Puddles have much to teach us about the way the land can be read and how deductions about the arc of the sun can be used to find direction.

Nearly all country tracks and paths have an incline of some sort on each side. Very often

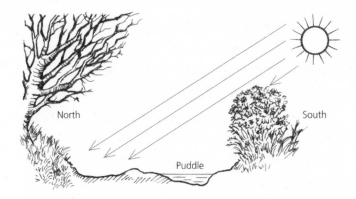

Puddles take longer to dry on the southern side of west–east paths in the northern hemisphere.

there will be some plant growth on either side [27] too. As the sun casts its shadows on the path, the position of these shadows can cause some parts to dry more slowly than others. A path that heads north–south will receive roughly equal amounts of drying sunlight on each side, since the sun rises on one side of it and sets on the other.

However, in the northern hemisphere the sun spends most of its time in the southern part of the sky. On an east–west path, the incline and growth on the southern side of the track will cast a shadow on the southern part of the track. Moisture is retained, puddles last longer.

Over time there is often a compounding effect. The next time the rain falls, the southern side gathers more water and the cycle begins again. In summer, the puddles may have evaporated away, but their effect can still be read in the shape of the dry mud and often in a shade difference between two sides of a path. Consequently, east–west paths can look very different to north–south paths and the junctions between the two will often reveal a stark change.

Occasionally it is possible to spot a difference between the ends of a puddle, from translucent muddy water to an opaque pale green at opposite ends. This can be caused by plant matter or algae being blown to one end by a prevailing wind. In the UK, the prevailing wind is from the south–west: the north-eastern end of a puddle will sometimes reveal a shade of green when the south–west does not.

[28]

The Plants

The presence or absence of sunlight has an enormous impact on the growth of plants, and this knowledge can be used for navigation. More available energy leads to denser growth and is therefore usually found in plants which receive more sunlight. This can be observed over vast areas of land or in the branches of a single tree.

Seen from above, almost the whole length of Sweden is dominated by spruces and pines. Spruces rule the south and pines hold court in the north. This has led to a booming paper industry and in some regions the sweet and sour stink of a paper factory announces that a town is near. On a smaller scale, the sunnier side of hill slopes will often have denser plant growth. One simple trick to remember in the northern hemisphere is that 'sweet is south'. Sunlight has a bearing on the [29] amount of energy a plant produces, in the form of glucose or sugar. This means that sweet fruits tend to favour the slopes that get the most sun.

Crops that stretch over uneven ground will betray direction. A field of rapeseed may come into brilliant yellow bloom first in the corner that has a southern aspect and some shelter from the wind. This will also be the corner that first reverts to green. These greens and yellows can spread across an undulating field to form a colour compass.

The effect of photosynthesis can be seen within individual plants themselves. Plants do not have a central nervous system, which means that their individual parts have to act and react

There are more flowers on the east side of the Giant Cactus of Arizona.

[30]   autonomously, so that each leaf, stem and branch can behave independently of the plant as a whole.

There are plants that react surprising quickly to the light. Heliotropic plants – those which track the sun's motion – like the alpine buttercup rely on getting as much of the low light as they can during daylight hours. Many plants display what is known as leaf heliotropism. The nasturtium leaf has an organ at its base which enables it to tilt itself at right angles to the sun and track it during the day.

Many plants show a preference for certain aspects, most typically between south and east. The flowers of the Giant Cactus of Tucson, Arizona show a predilection for the eastern side of the plant, where the sun reaches first and warms the cold air from the previous night. The 'North Pole' plant of South Africa (opposite), *Pachypodium namaquanum,* is a large succulent with a crowned head that reliably points north.

The Trees

Within most landscapes, the ideal tree to study is an isolated one. The problem with looking at trees in woodland, or even just two or three together, is that they will be reacting to each other as well as the elements. In a wooded area, always go for the 'King of the Jungle': the tree that appears tallest, oldest, most established and dominant. This is the one that is most likely to reflect effects of the elements in an unadulterated way.

[31]

Environmental effects are usually more pronounced on deciduous trees than on evergreens. Evergreens cope with low levels of diffuse light over long periods, whereas deciduous trees explode into action for a few months and their leaves tend to be much broader, which can accentuate the difference in light levels from one side to the other.

The most common mistake when studying a tree is to do so from one angle, trying to read it before you have taken the time to walk around it. A tree becomes many different trees from different perspectives and it is these differences that can reveal information about its orientation.

Try to ascertain whether the tree appears 'heavier' on one side. Imagine sawing a tree in half down the middle of its trunk and then weighing each side in a giant set of scales. In northern countries like the UK, the side of the scales that hits the ground will likely have a southerly aspect.

Next, look for shape within the tree. Reading a [32] tree is helped by an understanding of photo-tropism, the directional growth of a plant that is influenced by light. This effect is seen in branches on two sides of the same tree. The branches on the lighter side will grow out towards the light, while the branches on the darker side will tend to grow more vertically. This results in the 'Tick Effect'. When viewed from the west, northern hemisphere trees sometimes look as though they have a tick running across their branches (from the east the effect is backwards). While the denser growth can be spotted in the summer, the tick is easier to gauge when a deciduous tree's branches can be seen.

A third effect of the sun on trees can be seen after they have been cut down. Dendrochronology

In the northern hemisphere, isolated deciduous trees often show a 'heaviness' on their southern side and the 'Tick Effect' in their branches.

is the science of using tree rings to understand the age of a tree and the climate it experienced during its life.

A navigational pointer can be found in a different aspect of the trunk of a felled tree – an architectural one. If a tree grows more densely on one side than another, then it follows that the trunk will reflect this imbalance.

Trees cannot escape the wind, and their shape will reflect this. When looking for the effect of wind on trees it is the trends that are of interest. A tree can be blown temporarily in any direction during a gale, but its shape will reflect the prevailing wind in an area. Exposure is critical; a tree in the lee of a hill will often disappoint, but a tall tree on a ridge can sometimes be read from a long way off.

It is clear that the tree in the illustration opposite has been shaped by a wind that has blown consistently from the left, which in the UK means that south-west is likely to be to the left.

Clues provided by wind exposure can be found in fallen trees. Trees fall for many reasons but the final push often comes from the wind. Fallen trees in the same area that appear to have come down at a similar time are very likely to have been toppled by the same gale.

The prevailing wind shapes exposed trees as it combs their upper branches and extremities.

The sun and wind act in tandem. Isolated trees will often show a combination of effects, which can make the task of interpretation more challenging. It is worth remembering that the wind will shape things in proportion to how exposed they are: the outer edges and the tops will tend to show more 'combing'. In turn, the thick main branches in the body of the tree are more influenced over time by the sun. A dominant wind effect can make any sun effect hard to spot, but the sun's effect will never negate the impressions of a prevailing wind.   [35]

Mosses and Lichens

There is a commonly held belief that 'Moss grows on the north side of trees and buildings.' It does, sometimes, but it will also grow on every other side. Moss does not care about direction, but it cares greatly about moisture. If a tree or building receives an equal amount of moisture in the form of rain on all sides, the side facing the sun will dry out quickest. Hence moss is often happier on the moister, northern side in the northern hemisphere. The sun, though, is only one of the factors affecting moisture.

Gradient is important: the faster water can run off, the less likely moss is to find sufficient moisture. This can be seen on trees where a bend or hollow in the trunk can slow the movement of water and make a home for moss, even on the south-facing side. Texture is another factor; rough broken bark surface acts as a brake on water flowing down the tree and will likely prove a good habitat. Another issue is 'ground effect'. The ground retains moisture, which means that mosses often thrive close to it, [36] regardless of aspect. It is best to ignore mosses growing within sixty centimetres of ground level.

Algae are moisture-loving organisms often confused for mosses. They can be seen as a thin film, sometimes slimy in appearance, on bark, stone and other surfaces. Algae also give clues about the moistness of a surface rather than clearly indicating direction. They are visible as the greenish tinge to a woodland a few hundred metres away. The north side of woodland often wears this green appearance more noticeably in winter than summer.

Lichens are mosses' shy, more complex neighbours. They grow slowly and can live for several thousand years in some places, making them possibly the oldest living things on the planet. The route to navigational assistance from lichens is not through understanding their biology, but by learning to recognise colours and patterns within a local area.

The two main things to note are the surface that the lichen is growing upon and the effects of its environment. The aim is to notice consistencies, perhaps a light green lichen with dark speckles that favours the south-west of trees, likely enjoying the combination of some sunlight and rain-bearing winds. However, the diversity and [37] sensitivity of lichens means that a knowledge of local species and their features will usually be more helpful than an attempt to apply general rules.

The Towns

As with the natural landscape, there is a reason behind the orientation of most things in a town. It is the natural navigator's task to ask questions about how things are aligned and why.

Towns are not immune to nature. However great the leaps of architects and builders, the most ambitious edifices are still footnotes to any hills and rivers in a town. Occasionally there is a strong navigational heritage, but one that stems from the sky and not the ground. A perfect north–south line can be drawn in Beijing to line up Tiananmen Square, the Bell and Drum Towers, and Chairman Mao's memorial. This alignment can be used by the earthbound navigator, even if its inspiration was celestial.

There are marked differences between cities that have grown organically, like London and Paris, and those that have been carefully planned, like Canberra or Brasilia. The latter are usually easier to navigate, but less intriguing.

[38]

It is worth monitoring human behaviour in order to gain clues as to location. Railway stations can be found by going against the flow of people in these large cities in the morning and with them in the late afternoon. These movements are influenced by nature in ways that few give any thought to. The direction that people move will be shaped by time and that in turn is of course governed by the sun.

Natural forces are still at work in a town. The sun might cause colours to fade and paint to peel more quickly on one side of a particular street. The rain will tend to hit a building from the direction of the prevailing wind and stain it,

The sun might cause colours to fade and paint to peel more quickly on one side of a particular street. Mosses and algae will tend to favour one side of buildings too.

[39]

corrode it or encourage moss and algae growth.

Reading weathering is similar to reading lichens. By becoming familiar with local materials, and how they weather, one can gain useful knowledge about a particular city's weather and aspect. Corrosion or blackening will tend to be found more prominently on either the windward or leeward side of buildings. It is always worth looking up above the ground level of buildings as this is where the elements are able to work most freely.

It is sometimes possible to smell a river, lake or even a park before it comes into sight. The wind itself can be used as a navigational tool, even when the traveller is sheltered by tall buildings, by

The wind itself can be used as a navigational tool, even when the traveller is sheltered by tall buildings, by watching the clouds pass overhead.

[40] watching the clouds pass overhead. Prevailing wind direction often influences the broad layout of a town, particularly if there is a history of industry. The less desirable area of town is often downwind, the eastern end in the UK – hence London's East End.

A dependable modern indicator of direction is the TV satellite dish. These will be pointing at a stationary satellite and so will be consistent across large areas, often entire countries. In the UK, satellite dishes normally point south-south-east. Similarly, most tennis courts are laid out on a north–south alignment in an effort to minimise the effect of the sun's glare.

Religious buildings have always had a strong

relationship with direction. Christian churches are usually aligned west to east, with the altar at the eastern end. Mosques have a niche in one wall to show *qiblah*, the direction of the shrine in Mecca. It is also worth noting the orientation of tombs, graves or memorials. Many Christian graves are aligned east–west, in anticipation of when 'the trumpet shall sound and the dead shall be raised'.

The Sand

The hot and cold deserts of the world are renowned for their emptiness, but the clues that can be used to find direction are not nearly as scarce as the animals or people in these regions. [41]

When there is no sand in the desert air, visibility is excellent. This means that the height of the observer's eye can make a huge difference, and every opportunity to gain a little height should be taken. Even climbing on to a camel can open up a lot more terrain in front of you.

One key method employed by the Saharan Tuareg is the use of smell. The Tuareg rarely stop anywhere without lighting a fire and making a potent pot of sweet green tea. The clean dry air carries the smell of the fires over a long distance and can be picked up very easily if approaching from downwind. One way of finding a camp is to walk at right angles to the wind direction until you pick up the smell of smoke and then turn upwind.

Although generally unforgiving and potentially dangerous, the desert is a friendly environment to the natural navigator. Few other places on Earth offer such a clear, uncluttered view of the two pre-eminent navigational guides: the sun and the stars.

There are challenges associated with using the sun near the middle of the day in the desert, [42] since you will probably be near to the Equator, and the sun will therefore be very high in the sky near the middle of the day.

On long walks through plains it becomes instinctive to use your own shadow during the course of the day; over your left shoulder at sunrise to over the right shoulder at sunset on a long northerly trek. This friendly shadow is reassuring if the ground suddenly changes consistency or colour.

The effects of the sun can be used to differentiate between otherwise identical-seeming dunes in the distance. The sun heating shallower dune slopes will give them a bluish hue, making them stand out. When the sun goes down, the desert can become shockingly alien. But at night, the stars are a great comfort and easily found. In the low latitude northern deserts, such as North Africa, it is often possible to see both Polaris (or the North Star) and the Southern Cross simultaneously, providing a strong feeling of navigational security.

The lack of precipitation in the desert means that surface particles are not subject to erosion from water and can be left undisturbed for long periods. It is easy to find vehicle tracks in the Sahara Desert that date back to the Second [43] World War. If you are following someone on foot or in a vehicle, getting to know their prints will allow you to follow them easily.

In the absence of water, wind is the decisive influence over the contours of the desert. Trees and grasses in wadis and oases still reveal the prevailing effects, though it is important to differentiate between a prevailing wind and a sand-laden wind. Sandstorms might whip up and blow for a couple of days from a different direction. This can lead to conflicting clues: trees that bend one way, while sand deposited in the lee of grasses indicates a different direction. The method with the lee sand is very similar to that when using fallen trees in woodland: once you have established the direction that the last sand-depositing winds blew from, then you have a method that will work for many miles.

Sand and other particles carried by the wind erode the rocks that stand in their way, which can be seen in a gentle weathering effect or even lead to streamlined rock formations called yardangs. Facing the wind is a steep, tapered face that gradually gets lower towards the lee end.

Another clue worth looking for is colour. The [44] different colours reflect the different chemicals present in the composition of the sand, the varying levels of iron oxide in particular. This can provide a clue that one type is heavier than another and will behave slightly differently when blown around obstacles. In a few places this leaves a basic colour compass, pinker sand on one side and yellower sand on another side of a road, for example.

Clues to understanding the desert lie in its sand dunes. The dunes stand as a record of the relationship between sand, wind and topography over very long periods of time. If a desert has one prevailing wind direction, then the sand will likely form nice straightforward barchan dunes.

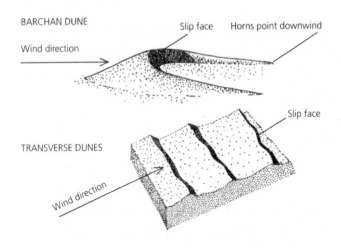

BARCHAN DUNE

Slip face   Horns point downwind

Wind direction

Slip face

TRANSVERSE DUNES

Wind direction

Some sand dunes yield clues to the prevailing wind direction.

[45]

These are crescent-shaped dunes with horns that point in the wind direction. A constant wind direction will eventually form transverse dunes, enormous ripples in the sand with ridges perpendicular to the wind direction, like waves in the sea. Converging winds can create linear or 'seif' dunes with ridges that run parallel to the mean wind direction.

A complex dune is created by winds that come from many different directions. They can consist of a mix of different dune types on top of each other, sometimes with a star-shaped dune on top. They are best treated in the same way as ranges of hills: they can serve as very useful landmarks even if their full history is hard to read.

Ice and Snow

The Arctic and Antarctic do not lack light but they never see a high sun. At such high latitudes, the sun's path is near the horizontal and so the change in the sun's height is so slight over time that even when it does dip below the horizon, it is more of a sunslide than a sunset.

[46]   The stars have a limited navigational role in high latitudes for two reasons. First, travel tends to be undertaken during very long summer days and, secondly, the stars themselves are harder to use: the North Star will often be too high to be a useful guide; the stars close to the horizon change bearing too quickly.

Wind and Snow

Snow and ice share a relationship with the wind analogous to that between sand and wind. There are comparable wave, ridge and ripple formations created as the wind sculpts the snow and forms regular patterns in the ice.

The wind organises fresh snow into drifts and lines with one end that points into the prevailing wind. Fresh snow is also deposited on the leeward side of any obstacles. In higher latitudes, jagged ridges, called 'sastrugi', are formed as the prevailing wind sculpts the snow and ice. These sharp edges align with the wind.

Another important clue is provided by gazing up at the sky in high latitudes. The undersides of low clouds will appear lighter or darker than normal, depending whether there is open water or ice in the distance. The Arctic plays with the [47]

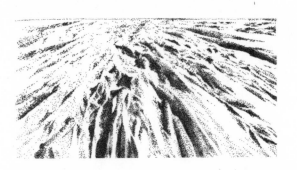

Prevailing winds sculpt ice into ridges called 'sastrugi' and snow often forms deposits on the lee side of obstacles.

light in one more way that can be helpful. Layers of differing air temperature cause mirages or 'looming', when the light refracts and land below the horizon 'pops up' above it.

CHAPTER 2

The Perfect Illusion: The Sun

Most people are familiar with one of the most basic natural navigational ideas employed by our forebears: the sun rises in the east and sets in the west. It is a concept that percolates through popular culture and has done for millennia. There is of course one small problem with this as a concept. The sun does no such thing. It does not rise; it does not set; it does not move within our solar system at all. How can two fundamental truths be so solid and yet so totally incompatible? As children, we are taught that the Earth revolves around the sun, but our eyes seem to demonstrate incontrovertibly that it is the sun that is moving.

The importance of the relationship between the sun and direction is one that was understood by everyone from the Phoenicians to the Vikings. In order for the natural navigator, too, to use the sun to find direction, it is necessary to unravel and understand the sun's habits.

The Spinning Orb

The Earth spins on its axis once every twenty-four hours. Each part of the globe experiences dawn, day, dusk and night as the sun comes in and out of view. The Earth also orbits around the sun once every 365 days, creating the year, but another piece to this jigsaw is needed before it can be used by the natural navigator. An explanation is needed for the seasons, a reason why the days are longer in summer than winter and why the sun never rises or sets in exactly the same place from one day to the next.

All of this can be explained by the fact that the Earth's axis of rotation is at an angle relative to its orbit around the sun. This angle is 23½ degrees. This basic mathematical truth delivers the variety in the seasons, and explains where on the horizon the sun rises and sets.

[50]

The diagram overleaf brings the words 'angle relative to its orbit around the sun' to life. Since the Earth is 'tilted' relative to the sun and because it orbits around the sun, it follows that during its annual cycle the amount by which each pole is angled towards the sun varies over the year.

When the North Pole is tilting towards the sun, the northern hemisphere is receiving more direct sunlight: this is summer. When the Earth moves half an orbit around the sun from a northern hemisphere summer, the season changes from summer to winter. However, after only quarter of an orbit the northern and southern hemispheres are neither receiving the maximum amount of direct sunlight nor the minimum. This is one of the 'in between' seasons, autumn in the northern hemisphere and spring in the southern.

There are four key moments in this orbital cycle. The first is when the North Pole is pointing as much as it possibly can towards the sun. In the northern hemisphere, this is the Summer Solstice, about 21 June each year, and it is the longest day of the year. A quarter of a year later, about 22 September, neither pole is

[51]

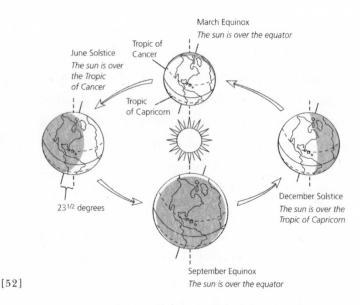

March Equinox
The sun is over the equator

June Solstice
The sun is over the Tropic of Cancer

Tropic of Cancer

Tropic of Capricorn

23¹/² degrees

December Solstice
The sun is over the Tropic of Capricorn

September Equinox
The sun is over the equator

[52]

pointing towards or away from the sun. This is the Equinox's mid-autumn in the northern hemisphere. Winter Solstice, the shortest day of the year, follows here on about 21 December each year. Round another quarter turn, on about 20 March, and once more both poles are perpendicular to the sun's rays: this is another Equinox, mid-spring in the northern hemisphere.

A knowledge of this angle and where the Earth is in its cycle around the sun makes it possible for the natural navigator to estimate the direction of the sun from anywhere on Earth at any time.

The Tropics of Cancer and Capricorn, the Arctic and Antarctic Circles and the Equator are all more familiar to us as geographical concepts than mathematical ones. These five lines of latitude wrap themselves horizontally around the world and although they have been given names, they would exist even if we did not, because they each reflect one aspect of the Earth–sun relationship.

When the North Pole is tilting towards the sun, it follows that the sun will be overhead a point nearer the North Pole than the South. On the northern hemisphere's Summer Solstice each year the North Pole is tilted as much as it can be towards the sun, and the sun is directly overhead the most northern point that it can reach on Earth. Over the course of Midsummer's Day this point moves around the Earth, and if it traced a line (think of a magnifying glass burning a moving mark on a globe) then that line would be the Tropic of Cancer. The same theory applies when the South Pole is tilted towards the sun: the line in this case is called the Tropic of Capricorn.

The Equator is the midway line between the two Tropics. It is where the sun passes overhead in mid-spring and autumn, the two Equinox

[53]

days. The Tropic of Cancer is 23½ degrees north of the Equator and the Tropic of Capricorn is 23½ degrees south of it. The Arctic and Antarctic Circles are the northern and southern caps where at certain times of year, near the solstices, daylight or night can prevail for long periods. The Circles extend 23½ degrees from each Pole.

This is the first, but not the last, time that it is necessary to reconcile a mathematical view of the world with a naturally observed one. Natural navigation regularly requires the observer to accommodate both approaches to one particular phenomenon.

[54]

The Shadow Stick

There is no better way to tame the sun than by watching shadows move. All that is needed is an open space that will not be disturbed for a day, and a stick.

Imagine that it is 21 March. At dawn, place a stick in the ground and look to see where the shadow from the sun is cast. Place a mark at the tip of this shadow. This can be anything: chalk, pebble, finger marks in the sand. Wait a while, then look to see where the shadow has moved and put a new mark at the end of the shadow. Repeat this until dusk and you will have a series of marks. Draw a line that joins these shadow tip marks together: if you have done a good job, the line will be a smooth, very shallow curve.

There is an easy way of telling when the sun is at its highest point in the sky and overhead your line of longitude. It is the moment that it casts its shortest shadow. Wherever you are in the world, the shortest shadow from a stick will always form a perfect north–south line and it will do this at midday.

[55]

Here is a shadow curve from 21 March. The shadow gets shorter over the course of the

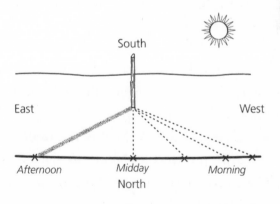

The tips of the shadows are joined to form a gentle curve in March. The shortest shadow will form a perfect north–south line.

morning and then longer during the afternoon. At midday the shadow is shortest and forms a perfect north–south line.

For natural navigators, midday is a literal expression. It means the midpoint of the solar day, the precise moment that is halfway between sunrise and sunset: the second at which the sun is highest in the sky. If the midday shadow is a perfect north–south line then which is which? The answer lies in that friendly angle of 23½ degrees. The sun is never overhead a point further north than the Tropic of Cancer. The UK is comfortably north of this, and so the sun has to be due south at midday, every day of the year. The shortest shadow will always be cast towards the north, the base of the shadow stick forming its southern end.

[56]

For countries that are south of the Tropic of Capricorn, like New Zealand, the sun will always be due north at midday and the shadow will point south. In the Tropics it will depend on the time of year: it will either be due north or due south (or conceivably directly overhead), but it will require some thinking about seasons and latitude to work out which.

Dawn and Dusk

Looking to the horizon reveals two very important times for the navigator: the start and end of the day.

The importance of dawn and dusk for the navigator can be seen by returning to the shadow stick and by considering the idea of putting aside a few minutes each day for a year to mark the points of the shadow tips (this is exactly what the ancients did, at Stonehenge and elsewhere).

The tips joined from one day will make a [57] curve subtly different to that of the day before, and over a year change quite dramatically. The

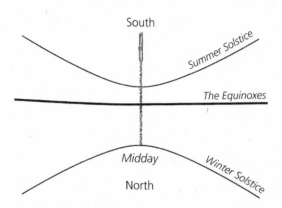

The different shadow tip curves over the course of a year. The shortest shadow forms a perfect north–south line every day of the year.

two extremes are the Summer and Winter Solstices: the two curves that lie on top of each other and fall in the middle are on the Spring and Autumn Equinoxes. These are the three lines which delineate the four key moments in the annual Earth–sun relationship.

The reason for the dramatic change between Midsummer and Midwinter lies in that 23½ degree angle again. At the Summer Solstice, the North Pole is inclined towards the sun. What this means to the navigator standing there, waiting for a dawn shadow, is that the sun is about to appear somewhere north of east over the horizon. Seventeen or so hours later, the North Pole is still very much tilted towards the sun and it will set with plenty of north in it too. The shadow will always fall in the opposite direction of the sun that makes it. The June curve will reveal that it has gone from a point south-west of the stick to a point south-east of it. In December, the South Pole is tilted towards the sun and so the sun rises and sets with plenty of south in it. At the Equinox, neither Pole is inclined towards the sun, and so it rises due east and sets due west on these days and these lines are very close to straight.

[58]

The shadows viewed over a year demonstrate that the popular belief that the sun rises east and sets west is both true and false. It rises due east and sets due west on the two Equinoxes, but not on any other day of the year. On the June side of the Equinoxes, from northern hemisphere spring to autumn, it will rise and set north of east and on the December side it will rise and set south of east.

There is another vital element in the equation and that is latitude. How far north or south an observer is does not influence which side of east [59] or west the sun rises and sets, but the amount. At 0 degrees latitude, the Equator, the sun will never rise or set more than 23½ degrees from east or west. In the Arctic or Antarctic Circles, there are times when the sun never sets or rises, because its rising and setting points have moved so far north or south that they have met again.

The UK's latitude is between the Tropic of Cancer and the Arctic Circle. The effect of the sun at either end of the day is less dramatic than in the Arctic and much more so than at the Equator. The sun will rise close to north-east and set close to north-west on Midsummer's Day. On Midwinter's Day it will be close to south-east and south-west. The difference between Midsummer and Midwinter's sunrise direction is about 90 degrees – huge.

There is no natural method for determining exactly where the sun will rise and set. This comes from local knowledge and experience. In an unknown area, it is possible to estimate the bearing of sunrise from latitude and season: to fix it more precisely it is necessary to cross-refer with other clues, like the stars (see p.108).

If one makes a study of the shift in position of each day's sunrise, the sun appears to move gradually along the horizon, but it does not do so at a uniform pace. Although the Earth orbits around the sun at a fairly constant rate, the point of sunrise races through due east at the Equinoxes and then decelerates at each Solstice until it appears to almost stop.

[60]

Approximate sunrise directions from Britain

NE	E	SE
Midsummer's day	The Equinoxes	Midwinter's day
June	March and September	December

The direction of sunrise and sunset changes more each day near the equinoxes than it does near the solstices.

The sun's movement along the horizon on the days either side of each Solstice is very small compared to that at each Equinox. Bringing this down to earth, the shadow curves change most rapidly in spring and autumn and hover around the same shape at the Solstices.

There is sometimes a temptation to think it extraordinary that the sun should happen to sit neatly on certain lines, like north or south, at certain times. It is, however, a false temptation, because the cardinal directions and the motion of celestial objects, including the sun, are just [61] different ways of looking at the same thing.

When we say 'I will head south', we are saying that we will head towards the sun at midday, not because that is how we will find the direction, but because that is what it means at its purest. The Greek word for north was '*arctos*', which means 'bear'. The northern constellation was the Great Bear (or Ursa Major). The direction and the object in the sky were not just synonymous, but identical. Although they had beliefs encapsulated in myth, the Greeks did not have a true picture of what lay in the far north: their concept of north was left in a purer state.

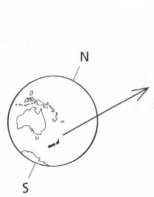

Sunrise in New Zealand in June.

[62]   *The Sun's Arc*

From a knowledge of the sun's arc, it becomes possible to do some direction finding. What direction will the sun be in the middle of the afternoon in the UK in September? The answer to that question can be found without any tricks, but by returning to the key points in the Earth–sun relationship.

September is the month of an Equinox. This means that the sun will rise close to due east and set close to due west. It will be due south at midday in the UK, as the UK is north of the Tropic of Cancer. The middle of the afternoon is halfway from midday to sunset and so the sun will have moved approximately halfway from south to west. The sun will be close to south-west.

What direction will the sun be one hour after sunrise in New Zealand in June? It is close to the June Solstice, so the North Pole is tilted towards the sun, and there will be a lot of north in the sunrise direction. New Zealand is south of the Tropic of Capricorn, so at midday the sun will have reached due north. One hour is only a small fraction of its journey from sunrise to midday so a good estimate is it will be just north of north-east.

There is another important aspect to how the sun moves which must be added to the equation; the sun's rate of movement. The sun moves across the sky at a uniform speed: 15 degrees per hour. This is the relative speed that nearly all celestial objects move when viewed from Earth, because it completes one full revolution every twenty-four hours (the equation is simply 360 degrees divided by 24).

It is, however, a more complex concept than this equation might suggest, because the sun is not usually moving parallel to the horizon. The sun is moving across the sky at a constant speed, but the change in its bearing is not, unfortunately, constant. An analogy would be when climbing a

[63]

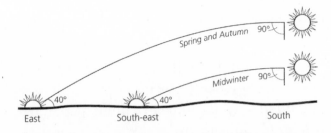

The sun moves at a steeper angle at the start and end of the day than it does in the middle of the day. This is how it appears from Britain.

mountain, even if the gradient does not tire the walker at all and they move their feet at the same speed, their speed in any one direction will vary depending on the angle of the slope.

[64]

The sun also climbs mountains and walks on nice flat plains. At the Poles, the sun moves horizontally, either above or below the horizon. At the Equator, the sun rises and sets vertically. What does this mean for direction finding? The higher the observer's latitude, the closer the sun is to moving horizontally, and so the more regularly the bearing of the sun will alter.

Difficult Times

When the sun is hidden by cloud, its light is still reaching the ground, otherwise it would be night: the rays are diffused, bounced around in the cloud before being released down to earth. However, they do still come from the same source direction and there is a straightforward method of looking for this. The trick is to use a long thin blade; it can be of a knife, paper, bark or leaf. If you twist the blade in a place that is open to light from all parts of the sky, you can often detect a fan-shaped shadow, which narrows to a line as you twist the blade and then grows to a fan again. The blade will point to the sun behind the clouds when the shadow is skinniest, when it is closest to a line.

[65]

The only thing to be wary of when using this method is that it will only tell you where the brightest part of the sky is. If you have an even spread of overcast skies then this will likely be where the sun is, but if the sky is uneven it can be misleading.

Hidden Tales

With practice, the outdoors can be read like a series of short stories about the sun's daily arc and annual journey.

The yews of Kingley Vale in West Sussex claim amongst their kind some that are 2,000 years old.

They drew me there one bracing December afternoon. On one side of the largest clump there was a clear frost shadow: the yews had been kind enough to play fat shadow stick for me. In the middle of the day, the sun had thawed the frost that it could reach, but not the ground on the northern side of the yews. The line from the centre of the trees to the curved edge of the frost was a perfect south-to-north line.

In the Alps, the same sun warms the glaciers causing the ice to melt, but it cannot reach every [66] inch of the cold ground. In a few places a large

Glacier tables.

boulder might act as a heavy parasol. The ice all around the stone melts away and it is left standing on a column of ice, proud and high. Eventually the sun will reach below the boulder and begin to melt the ice pillar, but it will not do it evenly. The sun's arc is to the south and so the southern side of the pillar receives more warming sunlight. The southern ice trickles away and the rock begins to tip and slip slowly down towards the south, bowing in deference to the southern arc of the sun.

The next time you spend a day at the seaside, plant your stick. If you join the mark from two [67]

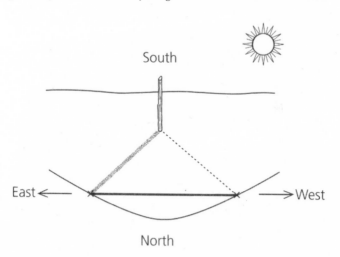

The tips of two shadows of equal length joined together make a perfect east–west line.

shadows of equal length in a straight line it will form a perfect east–west line. A coincidence? No, two shadows of equal length are just two moments equal in time either side of midday. It is geometry, which is another way of saying we have brought the sun down to lines in the sand.

CHAPTER 3

The Firmament

Popular understanding of the night sky has been slipping away since Thomas Edison's invention of the electric light bulb towards the end of the nineteenth century. Light pollution has obscured the stars from our view of the world and, consequently, our minds.

Despite this erosion of popular knowledge, the desire to understand the night sky has not disappeared. It is rare to come across someone who professes to have no interest in the stars at all, and learning to use the stars to find direction is an elegant way of reconnecting with the night sky.

The Celestial Sphere

The ancient Greeks saw the night sky as a celestial sphere encircling the Earth. While this idea has been disproved in purely physical terms, it lives on as the most effective way of conceptualising what we are able to observe in the skies above us.

There are approximately 6,000 stars visible to the naked eye in ideal conditions, of which only about 2,500 are visible at any one time. After taking time to observe them the following characteristics become apparent. The first thing that strikes most observers is the patterns of stars in the sky, or the constellations. Critically, these constellations do not noticeably change shape – from this we came to realise that the stars are fixed in position relative to each other.

Secondly, although the stars appear stationary relative to each other, they are not stationary relative to the horizon. Thirdly, the stars appear to rise and set in exactly the same spots on the horizon every single night.

Finally, at different times of the year, different stars and constellations are visible. Regular observations reveal the reason for this: the stars

[70]

appear to rise four minutes earlier each evening. The cycle comes back to its starting point each year, since 365 lots of four minutes makes twenty-four hours.

These observations and a lot more can be explained by thinking of the Earth as being surrounded by a gigantic glass sphere. Although this is now only a mental picture, to the ancients it was real. In the National Archaeological Museum of Naples there is a marble statue that dates from

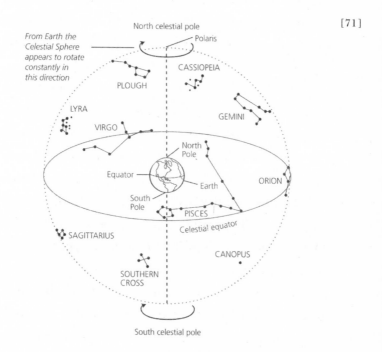

about the second century. It shows the figure of Atlas heavily weighed down by a sphere on his shoulders: a depiction of the heavens, complete with constellations.

The geography of the celestial sphere mirrors that of Earth. The points where the imaginary pole touches the sphere, the north and south celestial poles, are directly overhead the North and South Poles. The line on the sphere that lies above the Earth's Equator is called the celestial equator and as on Earth it divides the sphere in half. The sphere also has its own versions of latitude and longitude, called declination and Greenwich Hour Angle (GHA) respectively.

The sky that envelopes someone looking up from Earth appears as a dome. This dome is always one half of the celestial sphere. Its midpoint will be the point directly over your head, a point that is known as your zenith. Imagine that you are in a boat in the middle of a calm ocean with perfect horizons all around you. The angle from the horizon to your zenith will be 90 degrees, whichever direction you look. If you look up from one horizon all the way to your zenith and then follow the same line down to the opposite horizon, you will have looked along a full 180 degrees of the sky

[72]

– the half of the celestial sphere that is visible to you at that moment.

The stars appear to move, because the celestial sphere is in constant steady motion. In the celestial sphere view of the night sky, the Earth remains still and the sphere rotates around it once every twenty-three hours and fifty-six minutes. The sphere rotates clockwise when viewed from vertically above the north celestial pole.

It is easiest to understand the motion of the stars by looking at the extremes. At the North Pole, the zenith is the north celestial pole and only the northern half of the celestial sphere can be seen. The stars in the southern half will never rise above the horizon and become visible.

From the North Pole, the stars near the horizon appear to move horizontally from left to right, revolving counter-clockwise higher in the sky and around Polaris, or the North Star, directly over-head. The stars are slowly circling, some forming large circles along the horizon, shrinking to smaller and smaller ones closer to the North Star, which sits at the north celestial pole itself and does not appear to move at all.

The experience would be nearly identical at the South Pole, only there the stars move the

[73]

other way, from right to left near the horizon and clockwise overhead. At the Equator, the visible half of the celestial sphere will change constantly, with new stars rising vertically over the eastern horizon and setting vertically below the western one.

The way the stars move relative to the horizon will be determined by the observer's latitude and the apparent motion of the sphere. If your latitude is 55 degrees North, then you are 35 degrees south of the North Pole. It would be [74] possible to see some southern stars, in theory stars that are 35 degrees south of the celestial equator.

The critical thing to keep in mind is that the sphere is revolving around the celestial poles at all times, and wherever you are on Earth. An observer's latitude determines both which celestial pole can be seen and how high it will be in the sky. Standing at the North Pole, the north celestial pole is directly overhead. At the Equator, the two celestial poles will sit motionless on your north and south horizons respectively.

At a latitude of 55 degrees North, the north celestial pole will appear lower than overhead, but higher than the horizon – 55 degrees higher, to be precise.

The Celestial Poles

The celestial poles are invaluable for using the stars to find direction, because they are points in the night sky that sit directly and permanently over the North and South Poles. Even if you are in the Tropics and only need to travel a few miles, if you are heading north, you are still looking for a way to travel towards the North Pole.

The North Star

[75]

There is a prominent star in the night sky that sits very close to the north celestial pole: Polaris, or the North Star. It is a highly visible star, but not the brightest, which is a very common misconception. The reason for the prominence of Polaris in our thinking is its steadfastness, not its brightness. While all other objects in the night sky appear to move across or around in the sky, Polaris does not.

On a clear night in the northern hemisphere there is a simple method for finding the North Star, using a group of seven stars called the Plough (also known as the 'Big Dipper' or 'Saucepan'). First, find the Plough. This large group of seven

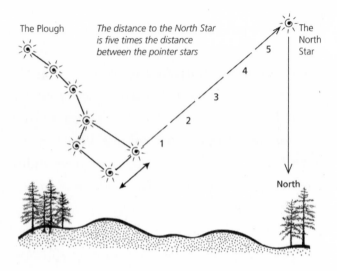

Using the Plough to find Polaris, the North Star.

stars is very easily recognised in the northern half of the sky, both from its distinctive shape and because each of its stars is bright.

Next, identify the two 'pointer stars'. These are the stars that a liquid would run off if you tipped up the 'saucepan'. Now visually gauge the distance between the pointer stars and look along the pointer stars to a point in the sky five times that distance beyond them. The star on its own in that part of the sky is the North Star. The point on the horizon directly below that star is due north.

Polaris is only the forty-eighth brightest star in the sky. It stands out because it is the brightest star in its patch of the sky. If you see two stars of similar brightness close to each other you cannot be looking at the North Star.

Polaris is less than a degree away from the celestial pole, meaning that it will always give a clear indication of north. A vertical line dropped down from Polaris to the horizon will be within 1 degree of true north. It is possible to make this line to the horizon accurately by hanging a weight on a string and then suspending it from your thumb with your thumbnail touching Polaris. This method can bring you closer to true [77] north than many people will manage to get even with a good compass or the help of GPS.

The Plough is close enough to the north celestial pole that it wheels around the North Star, never setting for those in northern latitudes. Stars that behave like this are called circumpolar stars. The Plough is what is called an asterism, which means that while it is a shape that is recognised in the sky, it is not actually one of the eighty-eight formally recognised constellations. It is in fact part of the constellation of Ursa Major, or the Great Bear.

The Plough can be used to find Polaris because it helps organise the sky around a familiar shape.

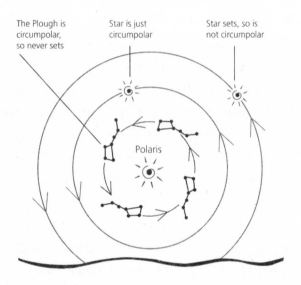

The Plough is circumpolar, so never sets

Star is just circumpolar

Star sets, so is not circumpolar

Polaris

Looking north in the northern hemisphere, the stars rotate counter-clockwise around Polaris, the North Star.

It acts as a signpost, confirming that you are looking at a northern part of the celestial sphere and pointing the way towards the north celestial pole. Although the Plough method is the most straightforward, there are many ways of finding north.

The constellation of Cassiopeia is also easy to find and lies on the opposite side of the celestial pole from the Plough, making it a good second option. It looks like a slightly stretched 'W' in the sky. Having found Cassiopeia, the next thing to do

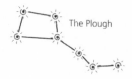

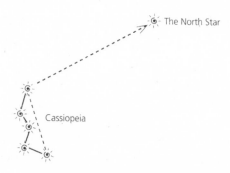

Using Cassiopeia to find Polaris, the North Star.

is imagine a flat tray lying across the top of the 'W'. Now imagine a line that runs at right angles to this tray away from the top left of the 'W' and double the width of the tray. This line will take you very close to the North Star.

The only ingredient missing in describing the location of Polaris in the sky is its elevation, its angle above the horizon. This is where the symmetry and beauty of the sphere really come into play. At the North Pole, the latitude is 90 degrees North and Polaris appears overhead,

90 degrees above the horizon. At the Equator, the latitude is 0 degrees and Polaris is sitting on the horizon, 0 degrees above it. This direct relationship applies whatever the latitude, anywhere on Earth. The north celestial pole, indicated by Polaris, will be exactly the same angle above the horizon that an observer is north of the Equator.

The Southern Stars

[80] In the southern hemisphere, there is not a prominent star close to the south celestial pole, which makes searching for it a little more complex than looking for Polaris in the north.

The Southern Cross is best thought of as having four stars, although there is a fifth present. At the head of the cross is the red giant, Gacrux, and at the foot is the blue-white Acrux. The south celestial pole lies four and a half times the distance from Gacrux to Acrux in the same direction beyond the Southern Cross.

It is good practice to look for the two trailing stars, Hadar and Rigil Kent, known as the 'pointers', to confirm that you have the right part of the sky and to make sure you have the true

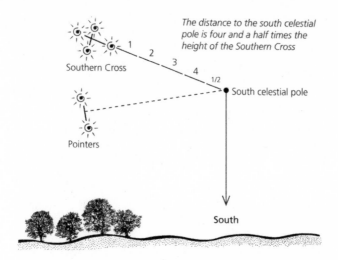

The distance to the south celestial pole is four and a half times the height of the Southern Cross

Southern Cross

1
2
3
4
1/2

● South celestial pole

Pointers

South

Using the Southern Cross and the 'pointers' to find the south celestial pole.

Southern Cross, not another group of four stars like the nearby 'False Cross'. As the Southern Cross wheels clockwise around the pole, these two very bright stars follow it. If you join the two 'pointers' together and then take a line that bisects them this line will also run to the south celestial pole. The intersection of the lines from the Southern Cross and this bisection gives a fixed point in the sky. It is not as neat a solution as finding Polaris, but it does work.

Rising and Setting Stars

If the northern stars rise and set north and the southern stars rise and set south, then there must be some stars that lie in between. The celestial equator, the line on the celestial sphere that runs above the Earth's Equator, intersects the horizon at two points for all observers: due east and due west. If a constellation can be found that lies on or very close to the celestial equator then it follows that it must rise and set east and west. And one of the brightest and easiest to recognise constellations does indeed straddle the celestial equator: Orion, or the Hunter.

[82]

Orion contains within it four of the nine brightest stars in the sky and it is visible to everyone in the world during last and first months of the year. Resting on the Equator, however, the constellation lacks the steadfastness of the North Star, rising and setting, moving constantly through the sky and susceptible to the seasons.

Orion's belt is used to find direction. The belt consists of an asterism of three bright stars, easy to identify because it is the only place where three such brilliant stars form a straight line. The belt as a whole rises in the east and sets in

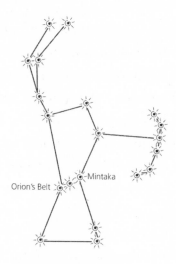

The constellation Orion.

the west. Mintaka is the north-westernmost of the stars in the belt. The northern aspect is important because the belt as a whole sits just south of the Equator, so the northern-most star is the one closest to the Equator. Its western aspect is relevant because it means that it is the one that rises first of the three. This means that the leading star in Orion's belt will rise within 1 degree of east and set within 1 degree of west.

Apart from the North Star and those that are circumpolar, all the other stars appear above and below the horizon at both different times of the night and year. So, for example, Orion is known as a winter constellation in the northern hemisphere; and a group of stars made up of the Navigator's Triangle, Deneb, Altair and Vega, is also nicknamed the Summer Triangle. The relationship between the stars that are visible and the time of year reveals another celestial calendar, as do the rising and setting positions of the sun.

The Planets

The planets are much less useful to the natural navigator than the stars. However, a basic knowledge of the planets is important for anyone using the night sky to navigate – not least to avoid mistakenly identifying them as stars.

The easiest way to distinguish a planet from a star is by appearance. The planets are a lot closer to us than any stars other than the sun, and this makes them visible as small discs or crescents when viewed through a telescope. Seen with the naked eye they can appear like stars in brightness, colour and shape, but the light we see is subtly different. Starlight is from a smaller pinpoint source, and as that 'point' of light hits the Earth's atmosphere it gets bounced around, causing the stars to twinkle or 'scintillate'. Light from the planets is from a slightly broader apparent source, and so even though it gets bounced around, it also averages out giving a more constant or steady light. Put simply, planets do not twinkle in the way that stars do.

The Greek word '*planetai*' means wanderers, and that is a fair description of the motion of the planets. Our view of the other planets is complicated by something called retrograde motion. This is an observational problem caused by the fact that planets that sit beyond the Earth in the solar system orbit the sun more slowly than Earth. In other words, their year lasts longer than ours. This makes them appear to move slowly one way in the sky, until the Earth 'overtakes' them on the inside and then they appear to briefly move in the opposite direction. [85]

The position that each planet will appear in our sky at any given time cannot be deduced by purely natural means. Although perfectly logical, the apparent motion of a particular planet is complex enough to require tables or software to be able to predict. There are, however, some basic principles that are worth knowing.

The movement of a planet in the sky over a few days is negligible, so once identified, their

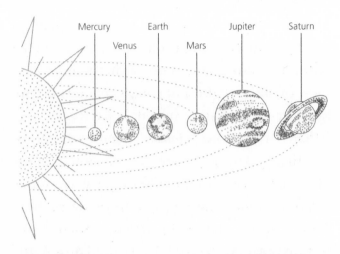

The planets in our solar system that are easily visible with the naked eye.

position relative to the stars around them will not change over the course of several nights.

The planets move in two distinct ways. The Earth's daily rotation causes all celestial objects, planets included, to appear to rise over the eastern horizon and set on the western. If viewed from northern latitudes then, like all celestial objects, their highest point in the sky will be due south. This arcing motion, from east to west, is the dominant one in the night sky, but it is not the same as the planets' motion due to their own orbit around the sun, which in turn is determined by how close they are to the sun.

All the planets orbit the sun within a similar broad band or plane, within 30 degrees of the celestial equator. However, only five planets are easily visible to the naked eye. These are Mercury, Venus, Mars, Jupiter and Saturn.

Mercury races around the sun in only eighty-eight days. This proximity to the sun makes it difficult to see in the sky, because it is usually blotted out by the sun itself. It will never be more than 28 degrees or three extended fist-widths from the sun, and can only be seen at dawn or dusk.

[87]

The brilliant white Venus is slightly further from the sun and therefore a lot easier to see. It is never more than 47 degrees from the sun, just under five extended fist-widths, but this extra distance makes it a much more significant feature of the early morning and evening skies. It is the brightest object in the sky after the sun and moon.

Venus spends about eight months of the year as a low bright early evening object on the horizon, before its orbit takes it in front of the sun and it becomes invisible for eight days. It then re-emerges in the early morning and can be found close to dawn for another eight months before it disappears behind the sun for fifty days and then the cycle begins again.

Venus can be a good ally for journeys once you have identified it. If Venus is a bright sign-post in the south-western sky one night, it will be there the next. The best way to use it is not normally as the primary way of finding direction, but as an excellent way of holding your course.

Mars is not very useful in finding direction, but can throw off your reading of the night sky if you fail to recognise it. A prominent red star close to [88] the celestial equator when you are not expecting to see one should stir suspicions of Mars.

Jupiter is the largest planet in our solar system and an excellent reflector of light, making it easy to spot. As it is another bright white planet, it is regularly mistaken for Venus. However, it sits far enough out in the solar system that its orbit around the sun takes considerably longer. Once found, it does not go anywhere in a hurry, taking a year to move through a constellation and twelve to complete the cycle. Like most of the visible planets, Jupiter can be used to hold a course even if it is not used to find one.

The yellowish Saturn is further out still and remains within one constellation for several years.

It is best known for its rings, but these can only be seen through a telescope. Its axis of rotation is tilted in the same way as that of Earth and so it experiences seasons, each one lasting seven years. It is rarely of use in natural navigation.

Shooting Stars and Strange Glows

The Earth's atmosphere is hit by approximately one million particles per hour that burn brightly and then turn to dust which settles over the planet continuously. These are meteors or shooting stars. Very occasionally, a lump from an asteroid will make it through the atmosphere all the way to the ground and qualify as a meteorite.

Meteors have a relationship with time and direction. You are likely to see more shooting stars after midnight than before, because this is when your part of Earth is facing 'forwards' as it moves in its orbit around the sun. At certain times of the year the Earth's orbit will take it through the dust trail of a comet. In October, the Earth passes through the trail of Halley's comet and so we experience the Orionid meteor showers, an increase in the number of shooting stars that appear to originate close to the constellation Orion.

[89]

Dust in the solar system can cause another light phenomenon known as the zodiacal light. A band of dust stretches out in our solar system in the same plane as the planets and when the sun reflects off this near dawn and dusk we can sometimes see it as a glow over the eastern or western horizons. The glow usually takes the form of a rounded triangle, with a broader base near the horizon.

Comets can be used like the planets to hold a course. Although it is popularly known that comets have tails, what is not so well known is that the tail will always stretch away from the sun, even if the comet is itself moving away from the sun. This is because the comet is not moving through an atmosphere and leaving a trail in the way a steam train might. Instead, its tail is being caused by a constant wind of particles from the sun itself. These same charged particles that push the comet's tail away from the sun also hit the Earth's atmosphere and leave their mark. The northern and southern lights, or aurora borealis and aurora australis, are seen as impressive arcs, bands and lines of green light with hints of other colours. They are most clearly visible at high latitudes, because those charged particles from the sun are channelled in that way by the Earth's own magnetic field.

The Milky Way

The light milky and dark patches that give the Milky Way its own unique fingerprint in the sky can be used as a celestial map to help us find other objects. A famous dark area called the Coal Sack can be found next to the Southern Cross and can be used to identify that important constellation.

If the navigational goal is of a more ambitious [91] sort, then the way to reach the centre of our galaxy is to aim for the southern hemisphere

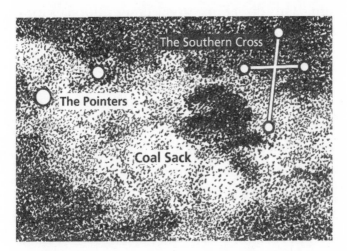

The coal sack can be used to identify the Southern Cross.

constellation Sagittarius, which can be found in the clouds of the Milky Way and looks a little bit like a teapot.

Time and Space

The relationship between time, navigation and the stars is a cosy one. Since the celestial sphere moves at a uniform speed around the Earth, it is possible to tell the time by looking at the stars. However, it is a bit like learning to tell the time all [92] over again, for three reasons. First, the northern stars rotate anticlockwise, so in the northern hemisphere the clock has to be read in the opposite direction to a conventional clock. Secondly, the clock is a twenty-four-hour one, which takes a bit of getting used to. And thirdly, because the celestial sphere and the sun do not move at exactly the same speed, there is some adjusting to be done to the time that is read off the sky clock.

It is possible to learn how to find north in under a minute, but do not let the ease with which you find direction allow complacency to creep in. The celestial sphere continues to turn after the sun has risen, but even the brightest of stars is quickly shrouded from view by the light of day.

If you are settling for the evening and find the direction you need clearly from the stars, then plant a stick in the ground and line it up with another stick, rock or landmark so that you can set off in the right direction the following morning. It is something you might be grateful for after the daylight or clouds have blotted out all trace of the stars.

[93]

CHAPTER 4

The Fickle Moon

There is both simplicity and complexity to be found in all things astronomical and the moon is no exception. Natural navigators need to be concerned mostly with light, time, tide and direction.

The moon orbits the Earth roughly in a plane from west to east and completes this orbit in a little over twenty-seven days. To make sense of how this appears from Earth, it is necessary to understand it in the context of the two other critical motions: the Earth's spin and its orbit around the sun. It might help to freeze the Earth's spin for a moment and ignore the sun. Now it is possible to imagine how the moon's orbit would appear from Earth. The moon would rise somewhere over the western horizon and move very slowly eastwards until it set over the eastern horizon about two weeks later, two weeks after that it would rise again over the western horizon and the cycle would repeat. This is quite counter-intuitive, since we are used to everything rising in the east and setting in the west, but remember that this is what *would* be seen if the Earth was not spinning.

Now it is time to let the Earth spin again. The Earth spins at 15 degrees per hour counter-clockwise when viewed from vertically above the North Pole. This makes anything in the sky appear to move from east to west at 15 degrees per hour – even if they are not actually moving. This is much faster than the apparent motion of the moon itself orbiting the Earth and so this becomes by far the dominant apparent motion. The moon appears to move from east to west, even though it is actually orbiting in the opposite direction.

It is time to reintroduce the sun. The two key factors to note are firstly, that the brightness of the moon is a reflection of the sun's light. Secondly, there are 29.5 days between successive

[95]

full moons, not twenty-seven as there would be if the Earth and moon were not orbiting the sun. This is because the Earth and moon have moved relative to the sun since the start of the moon's orbital cycle.

What We See

Because the moon's orbit makes it move slowly east in the sky, the sun appears to move marginally faster than the moon. If they are in the same place in the sky one day, then the following day the moon will have 'slipped back' by 1/29.5th of

The moon's phases and how they appear from Earth.

the way, or approximately 12.2 degrees (one extended fist-width plus an extra knuckle).

When the sun and moon are in the same part of the sky, the moon will not be visible at all. This is the new moon. Two days after a new moon, the moon has slipped back just far enough that it might be possible to catch one edge of the moon reflecting sunlight towards us. This thin crescent will be about 25 degrees behind, i.e. east of the sun in the sky (two and a half extended fist-widths).

One week after a new moon, the moon is one-quarter of the way through its 'lagging' cycle and this is called a first quarter moon. This causes some confusion, because we actually see half of the moon, the western half nearest the sun – the 'quarter' in this case refers to the cycle not the amount of the moon we can see. Fifteen days after a new moon, when the moon has slipped back 180 degrees, it is now opposite the sun. At this point we see the whole face of the moon as bright. This is the full moon. One week after a full moon, the moon is three-quarters of the way through its cycle and again we see only one half of it, the eastern half nearest the sun. One week later the cycle has come full circle, back to the new moon.

[97]

The key is to remember that the shape of the moon we see is influenced by how far the moon is round from the sun in its cycle. Since the moon lags the sun by a fraction more each day, it follows that it must rise marginally later each day. On average the moon rises about fifty minutes later each day, which is the amount that tide times lag the previous day on average.

Getting Practical

[98] Understanding the orbit of the moon and its phases is critical, but this does not on its own help with finding direction. To do that it is necessary to bring the moon down to Earth.

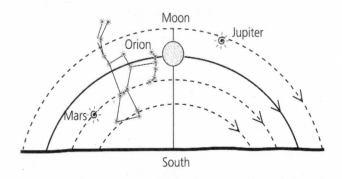

All celestial objects, the moon, planets, stars, as well as the sun, must be either overhead, due south or due north when they are highest in the sky.

The moon appears to follow a similar path to the sun and other celestial objects. It rises in the east and sets in the west, and at one moment it is neither east nor west, when it reaches its highest point in the sky. Harking back to what we know about the sun, it is logical that the moon appears at its highest point in the sky at the moment it crosses the meridian of the observer, that is the north–south line that runs from the North Pole between the feet of the observer to the South Pole. In other words the moon must be due south or north when it is highest in the sky.

[99]

A bright moon will cast a good shadow and a shadow stick can be used in exactly the same way as it is with the sun. The shortest shadow cast by the moon will be a perfect north–south line. If you are well into the northern hemisphere, the shadow tip will point north and the base south. Nearer the Equator, working out the orientation of the shadow becomes a lot more complex and it is better to rely on other methods.

When it is not a new moon and the sun and moon are not together, the moon must be roughly east or west of the sun. This means that the light side will point to the sun, which will appear roughly east or west of the moon. The bright side of the moon is acting as an approximate compass, pointing west or east. The best thing to do is to extend a line that touches the two horns of a crescent moon down to the horizon. This line will be perpendicular to the direction of the sun and any line perpendicular to an east–west line is a north–south line; this line will touch the horizon reasonably close to south if viewed from a northern latitude. This method tends to work best when the moon is high in the sky.

There is a third method, the phase method, [100] which encapsulates all the basic knowledge about the moon a navigator ever needs: its orbit, time,

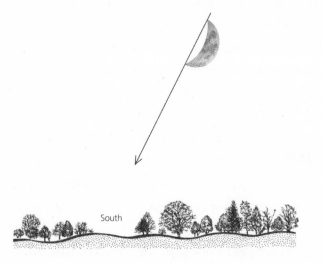

South

Using the crescent moon in the northern hemisphere.

light and phases. It is, however, difficult to grasp, and takes patience and practice.

To be able to find direction just by looking at the moon using the phase method requires three things: some idea of what time it is, the more accurate then obviously the better; an ability to recognise roughly which stage the moon is at, i.e. the difference between a six-day-old and a four-day-old moon; some basic mental arithmetic.

During a new moon the moon cannot be seen since it is hidden in the sun's bright glare, but if it could, then it would be positioned in the same [101] direction as the sun. That means that at midday the new moon must be due south from northern latitudes. At 6 a.m. the new moon will be close to east and at 6 p.m. it will be close to west since it is moving across the sky in tandem with the sun. So far, so simple.

A full moon is opposite the sun, which means that at midday the sun is due south and the moon is opposite it, due north. It is invisible at midday, because it is 'underground', but there are lots of times when it can be seen. At midnight, the roles are reversed, the sun is due north and invisible and the moon is now visible and approximately due south. At sunrise the full moon will be close to setting and therefore close to west and at sunset the moon will be opposite again, it will be rising and close to east.

One week after the new moon is a first quarter moon. A first quarter moon is lagging the sun by quarter of a complete cycle or 90 degrees. If the sun is west, or 270 degrees, then the moon will be roughly 90 degrees behind that or 180 degrees, which is due south (from northern latitudes). In other words a first quarter moon will be due south at about 6 p.m.

[102]   A third quarter moon is three-quarters of the way back round from a new moon. It is so far behind that it is actually 90 degrees ahead of the sun. When the sun rises it will be close to east or 90 degrees and a third quarter moon will be 90 degrees ahead of that, i.e. 180 degrees or due south. A third quarter moon is due south at about 6 a.m.

Things get more complicated when we look beyond those (relatively) straightforward examples. Let's try something a little more complex. Let's imagine that you are looking at the moon opposite at 9 p.m. The moon appears to be older than first quarter, but younger than a full moon. A best guess is that it is a ten-day-old moon. This means that it will lag the sun by about 10 × 12 degrees or

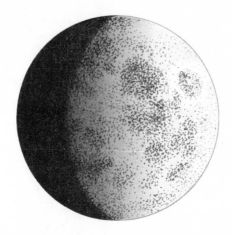

120 degrees. At 9 p.m. the sun will be roughly [103] halfway between its 6 p.m. direction and its midnight direction, which is roughly halfway between west and north, i.e. north-west. North-west is 315 degrees, so the moon is likely to be roughly 315 degrees minus 120 degrees, which is 195 degrees or close to south.

If this method seems fiddly and unwieldy, it will become far less so with honing.

The Moon, Tide and Direction

The extremes of tidal height and speeds are called 'spring tides', and they occur shortly after the sun's and the moon's gravitational influences

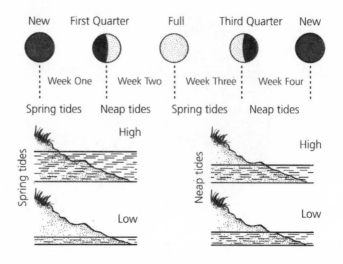

[104]   The extremes of tidal height are called 'spring tides' and occur shortly after new and full moons.

are aligned. This happens when the moon and sun are either in line, a new moon, or opposite, a full moon. Neap tides, the narrowest range, when heights at high and low water are as close to each other as they get, occur between the lunar extremes, shortly after we see half of the moon.

It is possible to refine this knowledge further and bring lunar direction into the mix. This is possible because lunar phase, time, tides and lunar direction are all interrelated. The height of tidal water and even its direction of flow are determined by the Earth, moon, sun and time.

With a lot of practice and perhaps some local knowledge, it occasionally becomes possible to look at a waterline and the direction of the water's flow and know what direction the moon will be.

CHAPTER 5

The Sea

There are many ways of understanding direction at sea that require no instruments, techniques that have been used by both ancient and modern seafarers. It is possible to enrich a sea voyage through a knowledge of these methods without throwing all the instruments overboard. They add an extra awareness of the natural world that can be enjoyed from the deck of a large vessel, in a small sailing dinghy or even by the fireside.

The Heavens

There are two broad approaches to natural navigation at sea, just as there are on land. There are clues from the surface, in this case the wind and the sea itself, and those from the sky. The sky is the first place natural navigators should look. If the weather allows, then it is often possible to garner more accurate information from the sky, at day or night, than in any other way.

The use of the sun at sea differs from its use on land in two ways. First, the use of shadows is not practical on small boats, since setting up a steady platform that does not rotate is almost impossible. Secondly, there are not nearly as many indirect clues available to us. The water [107] does not store useful information about the sun's path in the way the land does, and there are no plants that will yield clues. This means that the sun itself must always be used directly, particularly at sunrise and sunset.

To work out your direction at sea using the sun, it is very useful to know what direction the sun will be rising and setting for your latitude and time of year. If you do not have this information, it is possible, by following the methods discussed in the chapter about the sun, to make an estimate using an understanding of your latitude and the season. If you correctly employ this method, you are unlikely to be out by more than 10 degrees.

The sun is rising to the north of Orion and therefore north of East.

If you need to work out the direction of sunrise and sunset from your location from scratch then you will have to estimate it using the stars. This means having your wits about you at twilight, the only time when the direction of the sun and stars can be discerned in a similar time frame. At dawn, the direction in which the sun rises can be estimated by comparing it to the stars visible near the horizon. This can then be used to predict the direction of the sun at the other end of the day. If the sun rises a few degrees north of Orion's belt in the morning, then it has risen a few degrees north of east and will set a few degrees north of west in the evening.

The other method for working out the direction of the sun without the use of shadows is with time. If you have access to a clock, you can work out when the sun is highest in the sky, i.e. crossing your meridian, and therefore due north or south by timing sunrise and sunset and calculating the midpoint between these.

Knowing the sun's bearing when it rises, the direction it moves through at local 'real' midday and where it sets, provides us with three key points in the arc. The art of interpolation is needed to calculate all points of the arc within these three. Become familiar with the sun's arc and constantly test yourself against a compass or [109] tables until your confidence grows. It is possible to become consistently more accurate over the course of a single week.

The stars have been used by maritime navigators for as long as boats have existed. Here it helps to think back to the celestial sphere and how star movement is related to latitude. At the Equator stars rise vertically, at the Poles they move horizontally. The advantage of stars that rise steeply is that they hold the same relative bearing for longer periods. A star at the Pole will move along the horizon at 15 degrees per hour, one that rises east at the Equator will still be east of you three hours later.

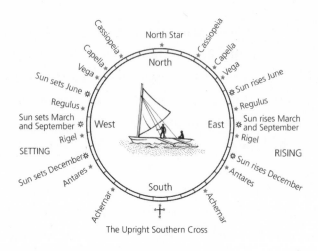

The Carolinian Star Compass.

[110]

The people of the Pacific developed a natural astronavigation system that relied on memory: each navigator had to memorise a sequence of stars for each course sailed between the islands. As each star rose or set above or below a useful height on the horizon, so the next one would be sought out. These 'star paths' would take the navigator right through the night. Since each star rose and set in a different place, the horizon was divided up into a sort of 'star compass'.

The star compass can also be used to navigate on land. If you arrive in a new village and the locals tell you there is a great restaurant five kilometres to the west, then you can bring the star compass and celestial sphere together by thinking of that restaurant as being one hour's walk towards the setting Orion's belt. You should be able to find it without a map, a compass, without even referring to direction itself again.

Reading the Sea

The sea may not reveal much about the sun's behaviour, but it can reveal a lot about what the wind has been doing. The following methods depend in part on some understanding of the [111] prevailing wind direction in an area. This is something that locals come to know well, but as we have seen, visitors can find it from natural sources on land, such as the trees. Out at sea, it is impossible to gauge what the prevailing wind direction of an area is; only what the wind is doing and has been doing recently.

Learning to read the sea to find direction starts with an understanding of the relationship between wind and water. A gentle breeze over a pond or even a breath into a cup of tea visibly disturbs the liquid. This instant effect of wind on water creates ripples and these die down quickly as the surface tension of the water dampens them. If a wind blows more steadily and strongly over water, then the water absorbs more energy and the ripples become waves. The size of the waves will be influenced by the wind strength, the length of time it has been blowing and the distance it has blown across open water, known as its 'fetch'.

Waves move forward, carrying this new energy with them. It is tempting to think of the water moving forward, but it is the energy that the wind has given to the water that is moving, not the water itself, which is mostly only moving up and down. [112] Think of the motion of a whip: a wave travels all the way down the whip carrying a lot of energy with it, but the whip never leaves the hand.

The energy that is carried in waves at sea can travel long distances, over 1,500 kilometres. When wave energy travels beyond the area where the waves were created by the wind this is called swell. Ripples, waves and swell are all manifestations of the wind giving the water energy.

Natural navigators are mainly interested in swell, since swell is more dependable than waves. Waves travel in the same direction as the wind, while swell will continue across or even against the wind. Swell tends to be less steep than waves, since all waves flatten and elongate as they travel. This is why waves sometimes break in open water but swell does not. Another effect of the greater scale of swell is that each crest and trough runs in unbroken lines. They are much wider than waves and run much further; often appearing to stretch out into the distance.

Even with practice, identifying the difference between waves and swells can be difficult. Lying on deck is a common method for detecting the rhythm in which the boat is moving on the swell. Balance comes into play too. For some sailors a change is detected when seasickness arrives after many hours [113] without a problem. This is because our inner ears are more sensitive to certain motions than others.

The larger the swell, the easier it is to identify and to work out the direction it is coming from. Storm-generated swell is the exception, and it bullies and overrides the prevailing swell. More typically the swell will have been generated by steadier prevailing winds, often blowing over great distances undeterred or molested by land. Although not guaranteed, the seasonal probability of wind direction is as dependable on some oceans as anywhere on Earth, because the effect of solar heating is far more constant over a large patch of water than on land.

The swell, like the trees on land, reveals the direction that the wind has been blowing. If a navigator knows the direction that the swell is moving, it can be used as a compass. The swell is dependable for hours and often days at a time, but not months or years in the way that the trees are. It is best to check the swell direction against the sun or stars. Then if the celestial clues are lost the swell can be used to hold a course. However, when the swell is used for shaping a course it is still preferable to pick a point in the distance to aim for. The horizon is rarely completely empty and a cloud or line in a bank of clouds will usually offer itself and work for a short period.

[114]

Swell will nearly always be used in conjunction with the wind itself as another means of holding a course. It is easier over very short periods to hold a course relative to the wind direction. However, the wind is less constant than the swell and it is possible to sail on a constant bearing relative to wind and come wildly off course, even in theory to sail a complete circle.

People in the Marshall Islands created stick charts as a physical representation of their deep understanding of swell patterns out at sea, but also the relationship between swell and land, in particular what happened when swell came into contact with islands.

When waves meet the coastline they are reflected off land in the same way that a wave will travel up and down a bath, bouncing off each end until all the energy has dissipated. The angle at which the wave reflects off land and the strength of the returning wave are determined by the incoming wave and the land it meets. Curved and gently shelving beaches will reflect much weaker waves than rock cliffs.

When a reflected wave meets an incoming [115] wave they interfere with each other and the pattern in the water, the height, shape and rhythm

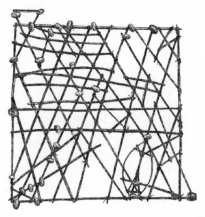

A stick chart from the Marshall Islands in the Pacific. It shows typical swell patterns and how these interacted with the islands. © Ocean Planet/Smithsonian.

of the waves will change. It is possible to simulate these effects on a smaller scale. By blowing gently from one end of a shallow rectangular bowl of water in which there is a rock 'island', it is possible to set up ripples that act as swell. By altering the strength of 'wind' and position of the 'island', it is possible to make out faint lines of interference in the water.

Beneath the waves and the swell the water is rarely perfectly still. If the wind blows steadily enough then currents will be set up as the water [116] follows the wind direction in a broad and gentle stream. Currents are also formed by differences in temperature and water density. In the Mediterranean the sun heats the water and

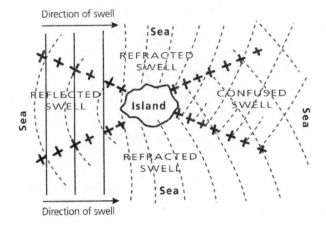

causes evaporation. Then the water level lowers and water tries to flow in to replace it from the Atlantic. However, the evaporation causes the Mediterranean water to have a higher concentration of salt and as a result it is more dense; as the fresher Atlantic water flows in through the Straits of Gibraltar, a deeper current of heavier, saltier water flows out below it.

The best known of the major sea currents is the Gulf Stream, which is created by the Trade Winds blowing across the Atlantic and flows north-east past the east coast of the US and [117] Newfoundland before crossing the Atlantic Ocean. Like all substantial winds and currents it is also influenced by the Coriolis Force, which is caused by the Earth's spin. This force acts on everything that moves over a long distance on the Earth's surface, forcing them to the right in the northern hemisphere. In the area of the Grand Banks, the submarine plateau rising from the continental shelf off Newfoundland, the warm current meets the southerly cold Labrador current and the mixture of warm and cold air creates one of the foggiest areas on Earth.

Knowledge of currents is useful not only because any boat, great or small, will be carried by them, but also because in some cases they can be helpful in determining position, by drawing a line in the sea. The Gulf Stream carries warm salty water at a speed of close to five knots and has a famous indigo blue colour which sets it apart from the other waters and currents that it passes, being particularly noticeable at its western edge where the clear line is known as the 'Cold Wall'.

The majority of currents are very hard to detect and so it is fortunate that they are weak, typically moving at less than one knot. Modern navigation relies on accumulated seasonal data, so that nearly all passages are undertaken through currents that are understood and factored in to the navigation, but that remain undetected. If a current moves a boat in the open ocean, the captain has very few natural means of detecting it.

In the Pacific, the Polynesians and Micronesians relied on experience and a practical method that works over short distances. By knowing that a destination island was in the direction indicated by two landmarks, it was possible for the navigator to gauge and assess the current strength and direction early on in a voyage and compensate accordingly.

This technique can be applied in any situation where two things clearly visible on land can be

[118]

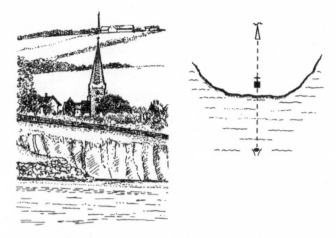

Using transits: when two fixed objects line up then we must be some-where on that extended line. This can be very useful on land or sea.

[119]

lined up. Imagine you are floating in a boat, with no engine on or sails up and in still wind conditions. In front of you a church spire is visible, lining up with a radio mast. Any change in that alignment will reveal what the water is doing beneath you.

The Tides

Even in this age of computers there is not a machine in the world that can accurately predict tides at a new location without the assistance of human observation. In tides nature has found a complexity to fox the zeros and ones.

The moon accounts for up to thirty centimetres of vertical movement in the oceans, the sun for up to fifteen centimetres, and every other effect is caused by the reaction as a body of water moves into shallower water and the intricate complexities of coastlines. These are the dominant factors, but to predict an exact tidal height it is necessary to take account of numerous other factors like wind, ocean currents and air pressure. An approximation of tidal behaviour is easy, but an exact picture is much more complex.

[120] Even if the science behind tides is well understood, there is still a gulf to be crossed in terms of being able to use this knowledge for finding direction. At its most basic, this means being aware that a high tide will follow about six hours after a low tide, and vice versa. This can help with the planning of short trips on coastal land or with the timing over shallow entrances to harbours. This logic works with the flow too: if the tidal water is flowing fast in one direction there is a very good chance that it will be flowing fast in the other direction six hours hence.

It is possible to refine this understanding. Tidal flow roughly follows something known as the 'Rule of Twelfths'. Starting at either end of the tidal cycle, low or high, in the first hour one-twelfth of the water will flow; in the second hour, two-twelfths; in the third, three-twelfths; in the fourth, three-twelfths; in the fifth, two-twelfths; and in the sixth and final hour, one-twelfth. Put a simpler way, half the water flows through in the middle two hours and so this is when the greatest rate of both water flow and change in tidal height should be expected. Shortly after a full moon you can be guaranteed a very high tide about six hours after a very low one. Similarly, if the moon is full or new

[121]

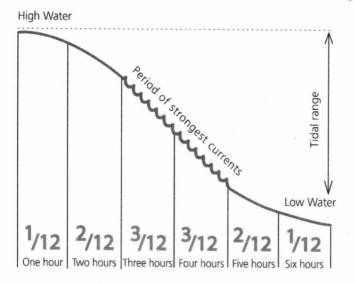

The tidal changes and current speeds are greatest in the middle two hours after each high and low water.

do not head out halfway between low and high tide if you wish to avoid fast-moving tidal water.

Another aspect to using the tides comes about through understanding the relationship between moon phase and tide. Sometimes this can be used more for fun than navigation. On holiday on a tidal beach, if you see a half moon in the sky, the tide will not reach anywhere near its high water mark, which means that there will be great swathes of beach that nobody is daring to lie on below this mark.

[122]

Colour

The colour of the sea is partly influenced by the reflection of the colours of the sky. But the water also absorbs some of the red end of the light spectrum. The combined effect is that we perceive the sea as blue. The effect of the sky's light can be seen most clearly during sunny days as small fairweather cumulus clouds cast shadows on the surface of the sea, giving patches of it a moodier appearance and reducing its blueness. This effect does not provide any navigational help. For that we look elsewhere.

Under identical light, not all sea colours are the

same. As with the Gulf Stream and Kuroshio Current with their dark blue waters, differences abound. The broadest effect is caused by differences in levels of salt in the water and the impact this has on micro-organic life in the sea. The general effect usually determines how blue or green the sea is: blue where it is very salty and green where salt levels are low. The Mediterranean is very salty and consequently low in phytoplankton, which gives it a rich blue colour. In the Arctic and Antarctic the seas are constantly diluted by fresh water melting from the ice and so organisms thrive, giving the polar waters a signature greenness.

[123]

There is another major factor in sea colour: water depth. The simple rule is that shallowing brings change, but it is possible to refine this. As blue water shallows over yellow sand, the colours will change as gradually as the sea floor rises from dark blue to blue-green, then to green and finally to yellow, by which point you are aground. The same effect but with different colours will be found over white or black sand.

It is good practice to carry a lead line, a weight on a string, which can be used to determine your depth of water with no batteries, software or salesmen attached to it. The technique of adding tallow to the end of a weight gives this simple method a dimension that the echo sounder still lacks, which is the ability to sample the seabed itself to gather clues to location.

The Birds

The historical relationship between birds and nautical navigation is strong. Captive birds have been used on board ships to sight land for as long as records exist.

[124]   Throughout history, the sighting of wild birds has been tied to an understanding of where land is, each area having its particular residents. The modern sailor, perhaps already familiar with the sight of Fulmars heading home at dusk, but wishing to glean more navigational information from the birds, needs to take note of several factors. These include species, number, frequency, time, season and behaviour. It is a vast subject but, with a little diligent observation, birds can assist the natural navigator.

Species is the place to start, because if individual birds can be identified and their habits are known then some general conclusions about location can be drawn. Flocks of birds are much more significant than individual birds, since solitary birds can be as eccentric as individual people, but it is unlikely that a flock of birds will collectively behave in a way contrary to their usual habits.

The first distinction to be made here is between coastal and pelagic birds. Coastal birds are more anchored to the land and so their habits can help the navigator. Pelagic birds, such as Petrels and Albatrosses, are oceanic birds, able to sustain themselves for long periods in the open sea and therefore offer very few clues to location. [125]

Since most coastal birds like to set out in the morning and return to land at night, it is fair to assume that a flock of such birds heading in a uniform direction at dusk are likely indicating the direction of land.

Landfall

Making landfall is one of the times when the risk of wrecking increases and so the navigator must be alert to all the assistance that nature can offer. It is fortunate therefore that where land and sea meet, animal and plant life, light, air and water all behave in particular ways.

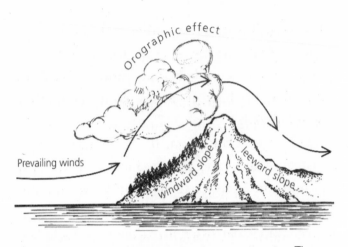

Clouds can be used to find islands before they come into view. The orographic effect makes the windward side of mountains wetter than the leeward side.

Landfall is not the moment of touching land, but of sighting it. Knowing this helps solve a riddle that has puzzled many. It does not matter how you travel: by foot, boat or car, there always seems to be a discrepancy between the navigator's estimated time of arrival and the time it actually takes to get there. The word 'landfall' is the key to explaining this. The navigator is focused on the moment when arrival at our destination is within sight or near guaranteed, since this represents the final hurdle in *finding* a destination. When walking it might be rejoining a known footpath that leads home and at sea it is the moment when land comes into sight: the landfall. There is always then a small journey still to be made.

One method that is used in the search for land is the scouring of the sky for anomalous clouds. Cloud is often formed over land by the orographic effect, which is when the landmass pushes moist maritime air higher, causing it to condense and form clouds. This is why the windward side of a mountain range exposed to moist maritime air can experience very heavy rainfall, while the downwind side is often drier, since it sits in a 'rain shadow'.

[127]

Clouds can also be used to find low-lying islands by looking for a different meteorological effect. The sun heats the land more quickly than it heats water, and warm air will rise in a column above the island, again causing the moist air to condense and form a cloud. A solitary stationary cloud, or even better one that remains motion-less over the horizon as others pass it by, is likely to be sitting atop an island. If the warm air is rising vigorously enough it can both form a cloud and then carve it in two, creating a tell-tale pair of clouds that resemble eyebrows.

It is not only the existence and shape of clouds that can yield clues to the whereabouts of land, but their colour. If the colour contrast between land and sea is striking then sometimes this can be seen on the underside of a cloud, a green tinge above a Pacific lagoon, for example.

The natural friction between land and sea can yield clues in the form of flotsam. Pieces of wood and, sadly, rubbish can appear anywhere in the ocean, but the incidence of these sightings tends to increase with proximity to land. There is one notable exception to this rule. Where currents are weak or converge, there are often stagnant waters which collect flotsam.

[128]

Underwater

Navigating naturally underwater is not as foreign as it sounds, at least not down to a certain depth. The same sun will penetrate shallow clear water and even give clues from shadows. It is also possible to use moonlight at night.

No diver is safe without a good idea of depth, and instruments are the safe way to monitor this, but light levels provide nature's best supporting evidence. It takes time to become familiar with the differences in underwater light. Both sun and moonlight are refracted by the water and so a lot of light is lost when the light hits the water from low in the sky, in the early mornings and late afternoons in the case of the sun.

The seabed has a topography in the same way that dry land does and the underwater natural navigator must be just as finely attuned to it. A diver can follow valleys, trenches and vertical drops in much the same way as the navigator on land.

Just as land which slopes down may indicate the direction of the sea, so the opposite can be true close to the shoreline underwater. The character of the seabed near land can also contain clues. As the water shallows, the wave action in the water creates ripples in the sand that run parallel to the shoreline. The tops of these ripples of sand will tend to be pushed over in the direction of the shore, like frozen waves.

If the waves are strong, then close to where they break they meet water that is moving in the opposite direction, having been reflected from the shore. This can create diamond-shaped ripples in the sand.

The most dependable underwater technique is the same as the first one we become comfortable with on land: recognising landmarks. Some of the landmarks may be unique to the

[129]

underwater environment, like coral pillars or kelp beds, but a few will be strangely familiar, such as submerged trees and even cars. So long as an object is unlikely to be confused with another and will not be moved by tides or currents, then it will serve as a landmark.

Underwater plants can reveal direction in the same way as land ones. They grow up towards the light, but this effect may be negligible when compared to the way they are combed by the currents. Instead of a prevailing wind, it will be a [130] current that leaves its mark. Kelp is swept in line with the current, whereas sea fans will be at right angles to this current.

CHAPTER 6

The Elements

Nearly all journeys undertaken by humankind take place within the thin layer of gases that lies between space and the surface of our planet. The Earth's atmosphere is not static, but is in constant motion as weather systems and winds whirl about above the surface of the Earth. The weather can influence the travel experience, but it can also be used by the natural navigator.

Weather is an important part of the journey. It cannot be divorced from the outdoors experience and nor should it be. For pure natural navigation purposes the weather that is arriving in a few hours or days is of less interest than what is happening in the present, and also what took place in the past. Grasses are bent by the winds of the previous hours, trees by that of the past years and the walker can use both of these while simultaneously feeling the breeze on one side of the face. The waves and swell of the sea reflect what is happening and what has happened, not what *will* happen.

The Wind

As we have seen, the wind holds an important place in the navigator's world. The sun, never far from consideration, is the prime mover of the wind. Solar energy heats the Earth's surface according to the angle of the sun's rays. Landmasses heat more quickly than the sea, creating warmer air masses. This in turn affects the air's pressure – warmer air expands, creating low pressure, cooler air forms areas of higher pressure. The atmosphere is in perpetual motion, as high pressure air tries to move into lower pressure areas. This creates wind.

The Earth's spin means that the winds never move in straight lines over long distances, the effect of the Coriolis Force makes them curve around the high and low pressure systems, leading to the trademark cyclonic whirls that satellites capture and forecasters like to prognosticate from.

There is a temptation to think of the weather as random, but of course it is not. The warmth of the sun is very regular and the landmasses do not change substantially and so it is inevitable that consistent patterns emerge. At the most obvious level, areas that get the least solar heating like the Poles remain cold and the Tropics are consistently hot. Dependable patterns emerge at a more [133] specific level, on both a small and large scale.

One large pattern, with great significance for Atlantic sailors, is the Azores high pressure

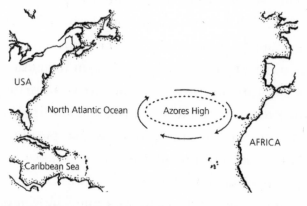

Winds circulate clockwise around high pressure systems in the northern hemisphere, like the Azores High.

system in the subtropical North Atlantic, which follows the sun north in the summer. The winds rotate clockwise out of the system creating the north-east to easterly Trade Winds that have carried transatlantic sailors from the Canary Islands to the Caribbean each year, and have done for centuries. The winds drive steady currents too, and it is often said that if you throw a bottle in the sea at the Canary Islands, you will find it washed up in the Caribbean in due course. The winds of lower latitudes are generally steadier than those at higher latitudes.

[134]

South of the Trade Winds are the notorious doldrums of the Intertropical Convergence Zone and north of the Trade Winds lie the Horse Latitudes, supposedly named after the horses that the Spanish forced off their ships into the sea when light airs delayed their voyages and led to water shortages. The global weather system becomes slightly more complex when there are knock-on effects. Norway and Sweden are not nearly as cold as other areas of a similar high latitude, like southern Greenland, because of the warm Gulf Stream.

Wind direction is something that causes confusion. The convention, which a lot of people

Winds are named after the direction that they have come from rather than the direction in which they are blowing. The top left wind in this picture is a 'north-westerly'.

find counter-intuitive, is for winds to be named after the direction that they have come *from* rather than the direction in which they are blowing. A northerly wind is heading south but has come from the north.

The direction of the wind can be used to detect broader seasonal changes, particularly in parts of the world with differing prevailing wind directions over the course of the year. A monsoon system is the most vivid example of this. Monsoons are winds that reverse direction in a seasonal cycle. In these parts of the world, like sub-Saharan Africa and southern Asia, wind direction is given a lot of attention at the change of the seasons, as the search for moisture intensifies.

For ancient sailors, who were unable to sail straight into the wind, it was crucial that they followed the right wind in order to reach their destination. Pliny the Elder described the French wind of Circius as the one that would take a sailor from Narbonne across the Ligurian Sea to Ostia. [136] Elsewhere, we find this method combined with distance to paint a more complete picture of the journey: 'From Carpathus is fifty miles with Africus to Rhodes.' Here Africus is the west-south-west wind that is needed to make the east-north-east journey from Carpathus to Rhodes.

There is another more fundamental reason for the importance of knowledge of the winds in earlier times. Prior to the compass, winds and their different characteristics were used to understand direction itself. The ancient Greeks noted that the south wind was dry and hot when it came from the direction of the winter sunrise (a little north of south-east) and moist and hot when it came from the direction of the winter

The Tower of the Winds in Athens was built over two thousand years ago and combined a weather vane, sundial and water clock.

[137]

sunset (a little north of south-west). The direction a wind had come from and the wind itself were one and the same, so that the cold northerly wind was called Boreas, but that word was also used to mean north.

In Athens there is a building from the first century BC called the Tower of the Winds, which beautifully demonstrates the holistic ancient view of the elements. The tower is an octagon and on each face there is a frieze depicting the wind from that direction. Boreas for north, joined by Kaikas, Eurus, Apeliotes, Notus, Livas, Zephyrus and Skiron in the north-west, as you move round

45 degrees each time. Skiron was named after the mountains to the north-west of Athens. There were also sundials on its sides and the Tower once contained a water clock for telling the time.

The characteristics of different winds can still be used to understand the relationship between the elements and direction. If the temperature or general feel of the wind changes, there is a good chance that the direction it is coming from has also changed. In certain places this can lead to smells that are associated with certain [138] weathers. In the UK for example, the coldest winds tend to come from between north and east, so if there is something to the north-east that emits a distinct smell, like the sea, its smell may give a clue to wind direction and even signal in winter that snow is on its way.

A sudden change in wind direction will likely be accompanied by a sudden change in weather. If you remain aware of wind direction you will quickly come to notice these trends. Small shifts in wind direction throughout the day are quite common, but substantial changes usually herald a broader change in the elements.

The reason for this can be found in the relationship between the high and low pressure systems, which bring new weather fronts with them. A weather front is the boundary separating two masses of air of different temperature and density. A cold low pressure front is leading a wedge of cold air behind it. The diagram below shows a typical low pressure frontal system and the wind directions that shift with each passing of a front.

Imagine that you are standing at point A. As the warm front approached and then passed over you, high wispy cirrus clouds would be followed by a high thin white layer of cirrostratus, [139]

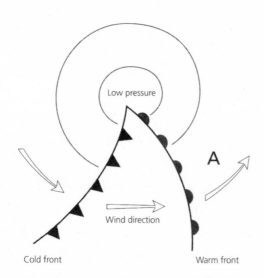

Low pressure

A

Wind direction

Cold front

Warm front

A low pressure system, with a warm and cold front,
in the northern hemisphere.

thickening as it was replaced by altostratus and then a big heavy nimbostratus blanket would cover the sky as a steady rain begins to fall. The wind would veer from south-west to west as the warm front passed and the temperature would rise. Then, as the cold front approaches the wind would veer to the north-west, the clouds would become more vertical and turbulent, the temperature would drop and heavy downpours and thunderstorms would be likely.

Winds blowing over an ocean will be marshalled only by the pressure and temperature gradients, but over land a compromise has to be reached with the land itself. Over broad flat plains the wind can march on regardless, but as soon as the land rises up the wind cannot ignore it and must find some way to accommodate it.

In the short term the land always wins, but over many years the wind has a great advantage. It is in limitless supply, unlike the hills and mountains. The windward side of a hill will show greater weathering and erosion, while the leeward side is where small particles like sand, snow, dust and leaves may accumulate. Once the patterns of the wind are understood, observations of weathering, or the lee effect, can be used to

[140]

work back to the prevailing direction and lead to useful deductions.

The best way to stay in tune with the wind is to use the senses of touch and hearing. Close your eyes and turn your head until you feel the breeze equally on both cheeks, and hear the buffeting sound equally in each ear. Having established when you are looking into the wind, raise an arm and point dead ahead, then open your eyes and look for a distant landmark. This will help identify an accurate direction for the wind and serve as a reminder for as long as it is visible.

[141]

There is not much point in asking the wind for help when it has been ignored for hours. If it has been acknowledged early on in the journey, its direction checked and compared with other clues, then it will happily repay this respect long after the sun, trees and topography have gone silent.

Every sailor must remain constantly aware of the wind direction relative to their boat. Sails that are set perfectly for one direction relative to the wind, or 'point of sail', will be rendered useless when the wind shifts significantly in any direction. One of the best known ways in which a pleasant sail is transformed into a life-threatening situation is when a skipper becomes too casual about a wind coming from astern.

When a wind shifts (or the boat's stern moves) from one side of the stern to the other, the boat may 'gybe', meaning that the wind will move from behind one side of the mainsail to behind the other. An accidental gybe can move the boom across the boat with speeds and forces that would make a cricket bat to the head seem like a good alternative to anyone in the way.

The sailor is therefore aware of the importance [142] of holding a course by keeping the boat on the same point of sail. A problem can arise if the wind direction shifts very gradually, so that it is barely perceptible. A sudden change in wind direction is unlikely and will nearly always be accompanied by other tell-tale changes in the weather such as squalls, but gradual shifts are common. For this reason the experts in navigating naturally using the wind, the Pacific Islanders, have learned the importance of constantly referring to other clues, such as sun, stars and swell.

The winds discussed thus far are those caused by large weather systems, but there are also local winds that a natural navigator must be familiar with. Land and sea breezes are caused by differences in the effect of the sun heating coastal land and the neighbouring sea. The land heats up more quickly during the day than the water and so the air above it also rises in temperature and expands relative to the air over the neighbouring sea. The warmer air cannot expand out to sea because the air there is cooler and denser, and it cannot expand outwards across the land because that air is warming and expanding also. Instead it rises and expands upwards, which leaves an area of low pressure in its place. This pressure gradient [143] leads to cool dense air from over the sea moving in over the land, creating a 'sea breeze'. At night the land cools more quickly than the sea and the process is reversed, as the winds blow from land to sea.

Mountains not only shape winds that pass over them, but can also create winds of their own. If the mountain is being warmed by the sun, then the air will begin to expand and rise up the surface of the mountain. This creates upflowing air currents known as anabatic winds. If the surface of the mountain is cooler than the surrounding air (for example, if it is covered in snow), then the air will become cooler and

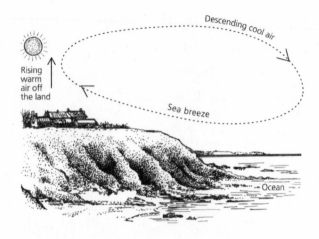

A sea breeze is caused by the air above the land warming and rising.

[144]

denser and begin to fall. This leads to downward katabatic winds.

The key is to remain aware of the wind direction and the weather more generally, even when they are not the primary means of navigating, and to tie observations of the wind's direction to other clues in the sky, land or water. The wind so often lives on even as the other signposts die away.

The Clouds

Clouds reveal much about the character of the air and its movement, like broad leaves in an invisible stream.

The exact form of a cloud will be determined by the meeting of almost all the factors that influence the atmosphere: the action of the sun, moon, water, land, air, human and animal activity. For most people, examination of the clouds is usually confined to looking at the broad types, since these reflect current and to a lesser extent future weather conditions.

Clouds can be used to give the observer a map of the stability of the invisible air. A blue field filled with a horizontal line of woolly sheep stretching as far as the eye can see indicates stable [145] air and fair weather. A tall vertical cloud must be caused by unstable, rapidly rising air and will herald unsettled, possibly stormy conditions. For the natural navigator, shapes are more useful than understanding meteorological terms, and when combined with an understanding of wind direction can be used quite effectively to give short-term forecasts. A constant wind and no vertical movement in the clouds promises more settled conditions than a wind that has just shifted noticeably and a horizon of jostling giants.

Longer term weather forecasting comes with both experience and an ability to identify the individual cloud types. It is hard to predict beyond the next few hours by observing a single cloud type, but a succession of different ones can give a fuller picture. Hence a cirrus cloud that in isolation may not mean much will, if followed by others such as cirrostratus and altostratus, usually presage the arrival of a front.

The next thing to consider is the direction of the wind you can feel and the direction in which the clouds appear to be moving. For the navigator there are two general levels of clouds and three levels of wind: the wind that can be felt on the [146] ground, the wind at the level of the lower clouds and the wind that moves the upper clouds. These three winds will more often than not be blowing in different directions, even if the differences are slight. This means that clouds at different levels will appear to move in two different directions.

The upper wind cannot be felt directly, but its effect can sometimes be read as wave patterns in the highest clouds. These are not the clouds that are normally thought of as 'weather' clouds; they are much higher than rain clouds, for example. If you look up into the region where aircraft contrails appear, you may see the icy upper clouds, such as the wispy cirrus. The upper winds are usually consistent with the prevailing wind direction and

The upper clouds are being blown from the west.

The lower clouds are being blown from the west-south-west.

The wind on the ground is coming from the south-west.

[147]

The three winds we can sense, ground, lower and upper, will regularly appear to come from different directions.

more dependable over long periods than the lower winds. In the northern hemisphere, the upper winds tend to snake from west to east.

The lower clouds are generally fluffy cumulus and blankets of stratus. Sometimes they are so low that they envelope us as mist or fog, the latter simply being extremely dense mist. The next time you find yourself in a mist, try looking vertically upwards. It is surprising how often it is possible to see up through it, sometimes even to a blue sky, or to higher clouds that might be helpful for finding direction.

More typically, the lower clouds are several hundred metres to a few kilometres up in the atmosphere. They will move at a slightly different angle to the direction of the wind that can be felt on the ground, which can be disorientating. Both the surface wind and the wind moving these lower clouds is coming from the same source, but friction causes the wind to shift in direction as it touches the Earth's surface. In the northern hemisphere it 'backs', meaning its direction shifts anticlockwise. Seen from above, the wind would appear to skid to the left as it comes into contact with the ground that slows it, because the wind is circling the centre of a low pressure system and as the wind slows it is pulled more directly in towards this centre.

It is important to be aware that the angle of difference between the surface wind and the 'weather' wind will be influenced by your location. Over water, where the friction is less, it might be as little as 15 degrees, but over land it

[148]

can be 30 degrees or more. Being aware of this can make the difference between a feeling of comfort and awkwardness as you feel the breeze on your face consistently disagree with the direction the clouds are moving.

The clouds can help navigators on both land and sea to find their way when the clouds loiter above islands and mountain tops, signalling land from beyond the horizon. 'May the peaks of Havaiki be banked in clouds!', runs one *fangu* or chant from the people of the Tuamoto Islands in French Polynesia.

[149]

CHAPTER 7

Creatures of Habit

We are the only members of the animal kingdom to have shown any interest in navigational instruments and yet other animal species seem to find their way around impressively. Animals can help us in two distinctly different ways. We can observe their behaviour and make deductions from what we see, but we can also study their methods and try to emulate them.

No animal is entirely independent of the others that share its habitat and whether we recognise it or not we are influenced by the behaviour of each other. It is worth monitoring the chain of animal reactions when moving across remoter areas. Some animals are notoriously fast at reacting and the slightly slower animals use them as a cue – mammals such as deer and rabbits will take flight shortly after birds have taken to the air. This ripple effect is one of the defining features of temperate wilderness.

Many of the navigational techniques used by animals are familiar to us already. Caribou and Wildebeest follow natural lines including rivers, valleys, lakes and ridges, while lemmings aim for mountains when crossing frozen lakes. Gannets have been removed from their home areas, released and then observed from an aircraft. They appear to explore the local area, searching for landmarks, before successfully heading for home. Released pigeons appear to avoid flying over water and to follow landmarks in navigating their way home.

Parrot fish, sand fleas, birds, beetles and bees, among many other species of animal, use the sun to orientate themselves. Some experiments have suggested that birds have an internal sun compass accurate to within 5 degrees. Bees are one of the most intriguing solar navigators because they not only use the sun, but they then communicate direction relative to the sun to

[151]

other bees with their trademark waggle dances. They are able to indicate the source of food relative to the bearing of the sun, the simplest examples being a vertical upwards movement meaning 'head towards the sun' and a downwards movement meaning 'head away from the sun'. But their dance messages are intricate and sophisticated enough to cover the angles in between. The idea that one bee can 'explain' to another bee how to find something naturally and more effectively than we might be able to is [152] extraordinary.

It seems that humans do not have a monopoly on the shadow stick method, since experiments with birds have suggested they use shadows to navigate. The stick in the case of pigeons might be a twenty-metre-tall tree, meaning that the angular change of a shadow over a short period witnessed by a pigeon could be six times greater than seen by watching the sun itself. Shadows magnify the effect of the sun's arc for pigeons just as they do for us.

Even the most impressive of animal navigators would struggle to use the sun at night, but animal journeys do not stop at sunset. Birds such as Blackcaps and Garden Warblers have confidently found direction in a planetarium and Mallards and Teals have also shown the ability to recognise the stars in order to navigate. The Underwing Moth not only orientates itself using the stars, but appears to focus its efforts on the celestial equator.

The bond between animals and celestial objects appears broad and strong. Underpinning this relationship in all cases is an understanding of time: some animals have an internal clock that is accurate to within five minutes over the course of a day.

[153]

The Birds

The ability of birds to reveal the proximity of land from sea has been known to sailors for thousands of years, but their greater influence on human journeys was probably in hinting at the existence of new land even longer ago. Here it is the annual rather than daily patterns that are of interest. Wave after wave of one species of bird heading out over the horizon with a seasonal regularity and dependability probably inspired and guided some of the earliest exploration and emigration.

It is interesting to note that the route used by the Maori fleet that sailed from Tahiti to New Zealand sometime in the fourteenth century and settled there is the same as that taken by the Long-tailed Cuckoo each September.

The direction and path of bird migration can continue to enrich contemporary voyages, but the modern traveller can also find inspiration from the birds in a different form, that of endurance. The Arctic Tern travels 18,000 kilometres from the Arctic to the Antarctic and back each year. [154] The main benefit of this extreme migration to the Tern and other avian long-haulers is the extra daylight for breeding and feeding.

The migratory endeavours of Arctic birds make them a logical choice for a deeper look into how birds find their way. High latitudes pose extreme challenges in terms of daylight hours, longitudinal changes and fluctuations in the Earth's magnetic field. Extremes often help with the process of elimination, and recent research is starting to unravel some of the secrets of avian navigation. One theory is that birds can navigate using infrasound, which is very low frequency sound, far below anything humans can hear.

There has also long been a suspicion that birds

have an 'inner compass': an ability to navigate by
magnetism, and physical evidence supporting this
has been provided by the discovery of the
magnetically sensitive compound iron oxide in
the brains of some species of bird. Birds are
believed to be sensitive to the magnetic field's
axial direction, strength and dip (the field's angle
relative to the horizontal), but not its polarity.
This would mean that they can tell which way a
magnetic pole is, how strong the field is and its
angle relative to the surface of the Earth, but not
which pole it is – i.e. north or south.   [155]

If iron oxide is the key to avian magnetic
navigation, then its presence might also explain
the navigational ability of other animals. This
compound has been found in animals including
bees, flies, bacteria, homing pigeons, dolphins
and, yes, iron oxide has been found in the
sinuses of human beings. An interesting picture
of the relationship between all animals,
including humans, and magnetism is building,
but it is very far from complete.

Radar tracking has led researchers to discover
something quite impressive about the routes birds
follow. Birds in the Arctic use the sun to find
direction, but not in order to fly a constant

magnetic course. Instead, they use it to follow a Great Circle, the shortest route between two points over a sphere. Calculating a Great Circle is a complex process rarely undertaken by humans these days without the aid of a computer. But researchers now think that birds might achieve this, simply using one problem as an elegant solution to another one. Their imperfect tracking of time as they fly on any course with an east–west component leads them to follow the sun in a path that approximates a Great Circle, which in turn [156] saves them hours of flying. It may be genius on the part of the birds, natural selection or Mother Nature. Or it may just be a lovely coincidence.

Birds can help us to understand direction even when they are not flying, since they like to congregate in sheltered spots and are habitual. Sheltered spots are usually out of the prevailing wind, which should get the deductive juices flowing. Navigating birds display an impressive adaptability. It does not seem to matter whether the sun or stars are visible, the terrain or magnetic field recognisable or the wind consistent, most birds will be able to use what clues are available to find a way to complete their journey. This is perhaps the best lesson for human navigators who attempt to emulate their feats: do not get too hooked on any one method because there will always be times when it is not there for you.

Insects

Spiders can give an indirect clue to wind direction in the orientation of their webs. Spinning a web is hard work and it cannot have taken long for the species to 'learn' that a lot of effort can be saved by not spinning against the prevailing wind. The lee of buildings and trees are [157] favourite spots.

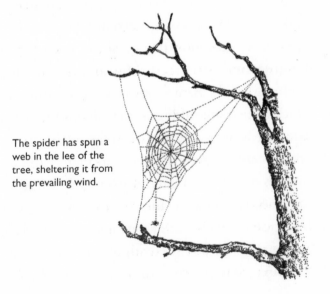

The spider has spun a web in the lee of the tree, sheltering it from the prevailing wind.

The Harvester Termite forages by both day and night and finds its way by both sight and by 'smelling' pheromones. If light levels are low, then it switches to sniffing its way to food. Logically, it seems more likely to use its sense of smell when heading towards food than away.

Bees demonstrate the importance of a non-directional aspect of wayfaring. Their dance not only indicates the direction of food, but also the distance to it. They manage to convey this by waggling their abdomen from side to side: the more wags the greater the distance. Experiments have shown that this distance is not a true 'over the ground' distance, but a measure of how far the bee will have to fly through the air. In still air conditions the two things are the same, but if there is a headwind then this will be conveyed as a greater 'distance'. This is something we experience regularly: we tend to overestimate the distance walked when travelling uphill, into a headwind or over difficult terrain.

Bees not only manage to navigate using the sun and to communicate this direction to their comrades, but they also manage to extrapolate where the sun will be from one observation to the next journey. They do not predict the sun's

[158]

movement perfectly, but are sufficiently finely tuned to it to understand that if their destination was in the direction of the sun twenty minutes ago it may be several degrees to one side of it now. If they are deprived of a sight of the sun for a period of hours they can still find their way using the sun, even though it will be in a different part of the sky.

The full list of navigational clues that the animals can offer would be a very long one, but two broad lessons can be drawn from observing [159] them. The first is that we are still part of the animal kingdom and therefore probably capable of a lot more than we suspect.

The second regards approach. Birds and many other animals have discovered, through natural selection, that navigation can be a life or death issue and that relying too heavily on one method is going to lead to problems at some point. This overlapping approach is a good one for human navigators to emulate.

CHAPTER 8

Where Am I?

Navigation is not just about working out which way you need to go, it is also about understanding where you are. Our position in the world and the universe is relative: if someone calls your mobile phone and asks where you are, you might reply 'London' if the person is in another part of the UK, 'Westminster' if they are in London but not with you.

What if you are somewhere with no landmarks? Latitude and longitude is the modern convention that is used to explain where we are. Navigators have always found estimating latitude a fairly straightforward business, while estimating longitude was a great problem until the eighteenth century. This is because the sun and stars behave with clearly observable difference as you head north or south, but they appear in exactly the same place when you head east or west.

Dead Reckoning

At sea, the lack of easy reference points meant that knowledge of position was treasured. Landmarks were valuable for coastal sailing, but once out of sight of land, the earliest sailors had [161] only three pieces of knowledge at their ready disposal. They could work out the rough direction they had sailed, they could make a rough estimate of how long they had been at sea and therefore how far they had travelled and, most critically, they knew where they had come from. This last point is often overlooked today: the ease with which we can summon our exact position at any time has devalued the previously sanctified knowledge of where we were at an earlier moment.

Dead reckoning became the difference between life and death at sea for thousands of years. The origin of the term is not known for certain, but it is popularly believed to be derived from 'deduced reckoning'. Dead reckoning is still taught to land, air and sea navigators, although its use as the primary means of navigation is waning. For natural navigators it is still an important method, even if it is employed for general interest rather than accuracy of position.

Hellish Longitude

Longitude and time are often described as being two sides of the same coin. If the sun rises one hour earlier for you than it does for someone else at the same latitude then you know you are nearer the direction of the rising sun than them: you are east of them. One hour ahead is 1/24th of the globe which is 15 degrees. A longitude of 15 degrees East means the sun rises one hour earlier for you than it does for people on the same latitude as you but at the longitude of Greenwich.

Navigators had known the relationship between time and longitude for centuries, but nobody believed that it was possible to keep accurate time at sea and so it was regarded as an impossible calculation. English clockmaker John Harrison gave most of his working life to

[162]

solving this problem by inventing the marine chronometer. His invention revolutionised and extended the possibility of safe long-distance sea travel.

This is probably the moment to concede that longitude is not a nut that the natural navigator can crack without instruments. If a concession is allowed in the form of a watch, then it is possible to roughly estimate longitude using a shadow stick, and then comparing this to a watch set to Greenwich Mean Time. If the watch reads 6 p.m. when the sun is observed to be at its highest then [163] you must be six hours west of Greenwich, which is the same as 90 degrees West.

Even the most ardent natural navigator ought to concede that the problem of longitude alone warrants the whole history of the invention of navigational instruments, while continuing to assert that the instruments are never more important than the journey itself.

Heavenly Latitude

The stars rise and set in the same place each day of the year, which make them a more useful means of calculating latitude.

If your latitude changes, you will see a different part of the celestial sphere. Even if you walk only ten steps to the south and then look up, the night sky will have 'shifted' from north to south a tiny and imperceptible amount. If you travel any significant distance north or south then the half of the celestial sphere and therefore the stars you can see will have changed substantially.

Wherever you are in the world the celestial pole closest to you will appear the same angle above the horizon as your latitude. If you are in [164] Sydney the void black spot that is the south celestial pole, which you have identified using the Southern Cross, will be just under 34 degrees above the horizon because Sydney's latitude is just under 34 degrees South.

This means that when you have identified the North Star (or south celestial pole), all you need to do is measure its angle above the horizon. To do this with accuracy requires the use of a sextant and practice, but the principle can be demon-strated very easily with no tools. The average outstreched fist is 10 degrees wide. If you are at 55 degrees North then Polaris will appear five and a half fist-widths above the horizon. On a clear night you can now find north to within

The North Star

— 1/2
—
5
—
4
—
3
—
2
—
1

[165]

An extended fist can be used to roughly gauge 10 degrees.

1 degree and estimate your approximate latitude in under a minute with only your bare hands.

It is possible to gauge latitude from the stars in more ways than one. At the North Pole, Orion and the stars on the celestial equator will skim along the horizon, moving parallel to it. As we have seen, at the Equator no stars graze the northern or southern horizons, but in mid-latitudes, stars circle around the celestial poles and some of them will touch the horizon as they do so. As they turn counter-clockwise around the North Star, the stars that graze the horizon will depend on your latitude. In other words, the radius of this circle is the same as the observer's latitude.

With practice it is possible to gauge your latitude by looking vertically above you and identifying a star that is passing overhead. If you know the declination (celestial latitude) of that star then you know your latitude. For example, if you look up and spot the bright star Capella directly overhead then you must be 48 degrees North as that is Capella's declination. It does not take long to look at a star chart or the internet to [166] learn a couple for your home and destination before a journey.

Keeping Track

The natural observer and traveller may choose not to view the world in terms of longitude and latitude or relative bearings at all. Instead, they may opt for general knowledge and general clues.

The ancients held much more stock in this general approach than modern geography can support. The philosopher Posidonius believed that the different bands of the earth, the varying latitudes, had not only similar climates due to the angle of the sun, but that the people in each would be found to be of very similar mental and physical character.

Knowledge of the behaviour of animals can help pinpoint location in a general or specific sense. Humpback whales migrate from Hawaii to Alaska each year and there is one place off the coast of Alaska that they hunt in teams, an incredible display that is not known to occur anywhere else on Earth.

The same theory can be applied to plants. It is sometimes possible to find patches of woodland that support explosive bluebell populations and this can help to build a picture, a sort of bluebell map, of an area of woodland each spring.

[167]

There is no limit to the interest that can be taken in this area, and the help that it can give in understanding where you are, in every sense. The possibilities are only limited by our own curiosity. 'Where am I?' is one of those questions that can be answered with a latitude and longitude, 'In a Kasbah in the High Atlas', or a hundred lines that take in the sun, stars, moon, planets, vegetation, animals, descriptions of the water and air and even the taste of the tagine.

Unity: An Epilogue

[168]

In this book it has been necessary to divide the natural world up into its domains. This is the best way to get to know the different faces of natural navigation, but the joy is to be had by experiencing it in everything we encounter in the world around us. We like to compartmentalise, it is one of our many coping strategies for the complex world in which we live, but sometimes there is more fun to be had by letting the divisions crumble.

If we head out on a clear night to look up at the stars, it does no harm to sense the breeze on our faces or to reflect how the clarity of the air itself provides clues as to the relationship between sun, air and water. The stars will not disappear if we pick up the smell of a log fire on the breeze and realise that this is being carried across from the village to the east of us, or if we hear an owl and note that he is in the woods to the south. The time we invest in trying to both fathom and observe the natural world yields a reward – an insight into the interconnectedness of nature.

There is delight to be found in esoteric connections. We can watch the long straggles of wool on sheep to confirm the wind direction, as the sheep themselves follow the shade of great oaks round the tree on a hot summer's day, like a clock and a compass.

[169]

On the shores of Chichester Harbour, on the south coast of England, there is a village called Bosham; the type of place that lazy guidebooks refer to as sleepy and pretty. I can remember visiting Bosham with my wife a few years ago. We walked from the church to a pub at the water's edge, bought a couple of drinks and sat, looking out at the scene of coastal perfection. I felt very little. It was undeniably 'pretty' and certainly tranquil, if not 'sleepy'. There was some small movement as a few kayakers waded out into the shallow water. All the ingredients had been assembled for a perfect moment, if such a thing exists, but instead I felt no more moved than if I were looking at the picture on a postcard of Bosham.

More recently, my wife and I returned to Bosham. We followed a similar route – it is a small village and there are not many to choose from. My face was picking up the subtle shifts in the breeze as we moved past a boathouse and then I strained to make sense of a strange curve in the wood of a churchyard yew, but failed. We [170] stood at the water's edge with our drinks, a metre or so from where we had sat years before, and looked out. The scene was the same, and yet it could not have been more different. The sun was dropping to the north of west and it arranged the land and water around us. The trees reflected the years of sun and wind. The first quarter moon pointed south and then ganged up with the strong smells of marine decay to describe the neap tide. The last of the sea breeze was greeting us and telling us that there would be a change soon. My senses fought to take in all the clues and my mind worked excitedly to fit the jigsaw together. I think my wife could sense the cogs whirring. She may have thought that I was worried about something and asked if I was enjoying myself. 'Yes,' I replied. And I meant it.

A few minutes later I asked her where she would like to eat. I followed her as she tracked the scent of fish and chips to the pub around the corner.

Sources and Notes

[172]

One of the aspects of natural navigation that either attracts or repels is the breadth and diversity of the subject. I have drawn from sources that range from ancient and modern texts, through my own experiences to conversations with contemporary nomads. Although it would be impossible to list every influence on my understanding and therefore this book, I have endeavoured in the following pages to outline where there are clear sources for facts, quotes or ideas. This is easiest when the ideas are specific and the influence limited; it is harder when a work or individual has had a broader impact. There are inevitably some ideas that have been with me too long to recall where they came from and whether they are original.

General Notes

Where no location is specified, a northern temperate location can be assumed, e.g. the UK.

Introduction: The Art of Natural Navigation

p.4 – 'A minimum of equipment and any available food is loaded…': Lewis (1972).

p.4 – 'When I stay in one place I can hardly think at all': I first came across this quote of Rousseau's in Minshull (2000).

p.5 – 'Aboriginal men': Baker (1981).

p.13 – 'much more sensitive to shape than we are to colour': Gatty (1958).

p.13 – 'Harold Gatty referred to the smells': Gatty (1958).

p.15–16 – 'the timbre of the echo gave clues': Beck (1973).

 – 'He watched them navigate their way in kayaks': Gatty (1958) citing Spencer F. Chapman from 'On Not Getting Lost'. *The Boys' Country Book* (Editor. John Moore). Collins, 1955. Pages 39–48.

p.16 'songlines': For more on this, see Bruce Chatwin's *Songlines*. Vintage, 1998.

– 'A lot could be written on the delight of setting foot on rock': Spufford (2008) quoting Scott (1913).

p.18 – 'kinaesthetic': Baker (1981).

p.19 – 'a ten-minute error per twenty-four hours': 'An Experiment in Temporal Disorientation'. *ACTA Psychologica 1* (1935). Macleod and Roff.

– 'Gwi tribe measure time in days and fractions of days': Silberbauer (1981).

[174]   p.20 – 'We are at Number Fourteen Pony Camp': Scott (1913).

Chapter 1 – Vale and Dune: The Land

p.25 – The habits of burrowing animals were brought to my attention by David Langmead during a course at West Dean College.

p.26 – 'drumlins': this was flagged by Nick Veck during a course.

p.30 – 'heliotropic plants': Galen, Candace. 'Sun Stalkers'. *Natural History*, May 1999.

p.30–31 'Giant Cactus of Tucson': Johnson, D.S. 'The Distribution and Succession of the Flowers of the Giant Cactus in Relation to Isolation' in 'The American Association for the

Advancement of Science Section G, Botany'.
Science. 42: 874880 17 December 1915,

p.38 –'Tiananmen Square': Aveni (2008).

p.44–46 – sand dunes: for the defining work on the behaviour of sand in the desert, see Bagnold (1941).

Chapter 2 – The Perfect Illusion: The Sun

p.54 – 'The Shadow Stick': I first came across shadow stick methods in outdoor and survival literature, but through experimenting and reading around the subject discovered that [175] the survival approach usually only touches the surface. I can recommend *The History and Practice of Ancient Astronomy* by James Evans (1998), *Ancient Astronomy* by Clive Ruggles (2005) and *Astronomy Before the Telescope,* Editor Christopher Walker (1996).

p.66–67 – 'sun warms the glaciers': Gatty (1958).

Chapter 3 – The Firmament

p.70 – 'constellations do not noticeably change shape': the stars are moving and moving quickly and therefore the constellations do change shape, but not noticeably over several lifetimes, only over thousands of years.

p.73 – 'the North Star, which . . . does not appear to move at all': Polaris, the North Star, is situated very close to the north celestial pole, but not exactly on it. It therefore does move, tracing a tiny circle around the pole.

p.80 – Star names: the names referred to in this chapter come from varied sources but two good places to look for ancient or mythological references are *Star Names, Their Lore and Meaning* by Richard Hinckley Allen (1963) and *People and the Sky* by Anthony Aveni (2008).

[176]

Chapter 4 – The Fickle Moon

p.94 – 'The moon orbits the Earth': The moon is Earth's nearest neighbour and while it is convenient to say that it orbits the Earth, this is an oversimplification. The proximity and size of the moon mean that it exerts a sufficiently large gravitational pull on the Earth that they actually orbit each other; in fact, they both orbit around a point in the Earth known as the barycentre, about 4,700km from the centre of the Earth on a line from the centre of the Earth towards the moon.

Chapter 5 – The Sea

p.107 – 'make an estimate using an understanding of your latitude and the season': This requires an understanding of all the principles in chapter two, and some practice.

p.112 – 'Think of the motion of a whip': this lovely analogy is Jack Lagan's from *The Barefoot Navigator* (2006).

p.113 – 'each crest and trough runs in unbroken lines': Burch (2008).

p. 119–121 – For a thorough analysis of the tides see McCully (2006).

p.123 – 'giving polar waters a signature greenness': Gatty (1958).

p.128 – 'Underwater': My diving experience is limited to the PADI Advanced Open Water Diver course. The 'Underwater' section relies on the following sources:

a) Personal correspondence with Charles Bennett.

b) *Underwater Navigation* by Ralph D. Erickson. PADI. 1979

c) *How to Find Your Way: A Complete Guide to Underwater Navigation* by Jim Foley. Dacor Corporation, 1979.

Chapter 6 – The Elements

p.138 – 'something to the north-east that emits a distinct smell': Rachel Donaldson, in a conversation during an outdoor course, explained that she could tell when it was going to snow at her home because the smell of Medway power station came in from the north-east.

Chapter 7 – Creatures of Habit

p.151 – 'Caribou and Wildebeest follow natural lines… lemmings': Baker (1981).

[178]

– 'Gannets': *Encyclopedia Britannica 2009 Ultimate Reference Suite.*

p.151–153 – 'Bees are one of the most intriguing solar navigators . . .': Gould (1980) and Gekakis (1998).

p.152 – 'angular change of a shadow': Galler, Schmidt-Koenig, Jacobs and Belleville (2005).

p.153 – 'some animals have an internal clock': Baker (1981).

p.154 – 'birds can navigate using infrasound': Jonathan Hagstrum Frin, personal conversation.

p.155 – 'Iron oxide has been found in the sinuses of human beings': Baker, Mather and Kennaugh (1983).

p.156 – 'a path that approximates a Great Circle':
Qiu (2005).

– '[Birds] like to congregate in sheltered spots':
Gatty (1958).

p.158 – 'The Harvester Termite': Leuthold, R.H.,
O. Bruinsma and A. Van Huis (1976).

– 'Bees not only manage to navigate using the
sun . . .': Gould (1980).

Bibliography

[180] Allen, Richard Hinckley. *Star Names, Their Lore and Meaning*. Dover Publications, Inc, 1963.

Aveni, Anthony. *People and the Sky*. Thames and Hudson, 2008.

Baker, Robin, R. *Human Navigation and the Sixth Sense*. Simon and Schuster, 1981.

Baker, Robin R., Janice G. Mather & John H. Kennaugh. 'Magnetic Bones in Human Sinuses'. *Nature*. 301 (1983): 78–80.

Beck, Horace. *Folklore and the Sea*. Published for the Marine Historical Association by Wesleyan University Press, 1973.

Burch, David. *Emergency Navigation.* International Marine, 2008.

Creamer, Marvin. *The Globe Star Voyage.* Unpublished, 1985.

Evans, James. *The History and Practice of Ancient Astronomy.* Oxford University Press, 1998.

Erickson, Ralph D. *Underwater Navigation.* PADI, 1979.

Foley, Jim. *How to Find Your Way: A Complete Guide to Underwater Navigation.* Dacor Corporation, 1979. [181]

Galler, Sidney R., Klaus Schmidt-Koenig, George J. Jacons & Richard E. Belleville (Editors). *Animal Orientation and Navigation.* University Press of the Pacific, 2005.

Gatty, Harold. *Nature is Your Guide: How to Find Your Way on Land and Sea.* Collins, 1958.

Gekakis, Nicholas. 'Circadian Mechanism Role of the CLOCK Protein in the Mammalian'. *Science.* 290: 1564 (1998).

Gould, James. 'Sun Compensation by Bees'. *Science.* 207: 44301 (1980): 545–547

Kolbert, Elizabeth (Editor). *The Arctic: An Anthology.* Granta, 2008.

Kunitzsch, Paul, and Tim Smart. *A Dictionary of Modern Star Names.* Sky Publishing, 2006.

Lagan, Jack. *The Barefoot Navigator.* Adlard Coles Nautical, 2006.

[182] Leuthold, R. H., O. Bruinsma & A. Van Huis. 'Optical and Pheromonal Orientation and Memory for Homing Distance in the Harvester Termite Hodotermes mossambicus (Hagen)'; *Behavioral Ecology and Sociobiology.* 1:2 (1976): 127–139.

Lewis, David. *The Voyaging Stars.* Fontana/ Collins, 1978.

Lewis, David. *We, the Navigators.* University of Hawaii Press, 1972.

McCully, James Greig. *Beyond the Moon.* World Scientific Publishing Co. Pte. Ltd, 2006.

Minshull, Duncan (Editor). *The Vintage Book of*

Walking. Vintage, 2000.

Qiu, Jane. 'Ornithology: Flight of the Navigators'. *Nature.* 437 (2005): 804–806.

Ruggles, Clive. *Ancient Astronomy, An Encyclopedia of Cosmologies and Myth.* ABCCLIO Ltd, 2005.

Scott, Robert Falcon. *Scott's Last Expedition.* Smith, Elder, 1913.

Silberbauer, George B. *Hunter and Habitat in the Central Kalahari.* Cambridge University Press, 1981.

Spufford, Francis (Editor). *The Antarctic: An Anthology.* Granta Publications, 2008.

Acknowledgements

[184] I would like to thank the following people for sharing (and enduring) the zeal that has been necessary to take this book from an idea to reality.

My family, not least my wife, sister, brother and father for their input and support. My agent, Sophie Hicks; and Louisa Joyner, Toby Clarke and all the team at Virgin Books for working so tirelessly with me on the book from its conception. I would also like to thank Clare Wallis and Tom Bromley for their work on this abridged edition. Margaret Stead, Ruth Murray, Fiona Vincent, David Burch, Marvin Creamer and Tom Peppitt for playing vital roles towards the end. The many instructors, friends and colleagues who have, over the years, shared the risks and helped shape my passion for navigation. David Palmer for serendipity and John Haggarty of South Stoke for inspiration.

I would also like to thank all those who have come on my natural navigation courses – this book would not have been possible without you.

[185]

Index

[191]

[194]